David Tomás

THE HAPPIEST COMPANY IN THE WORLD

Eleven Keys to Reinventing Your Job and
Enjoying Your Work

Contents

1. The message 3
2. Captain Flint 8
3. John Silver 11
4. Simon's report 15
5. The Crew 19
6. The first meeting 23
7. The binary test 27
8. Balancing out 31
9. Breaking the news 36
10. A place for everyone 39
11. A "Wow" experience 43
12. Green for happiness 46
13. A meeting for happiness 49
14. First values meeting 52
15. A great idea 56
16. Recruitment begins 60
17. The phone interview 63

18. Virtuous circle 66

19. Green for happiness (II) 70

20. More interviews 73

21. The new cabin boy 78

22. Yes or No 82

23. Happy reading 86

24. Flight of the geese 88

25. The quoting game 93

26. The fourth value 96

27. The Loewenstein experiment 100

28. Christmas Eve 104

29. Holding hands 109

30. Happiness is a puzzle 112

31. The nomination 116

32. Steaming with ideas 120

33. Life-changing books...124

34. Twelve 128

35. The happiest bookshop in the world..132

Epilogue: digging up the treasure..135

The happiest company in the world

1.
The message

The propellers of the old airplane whirled as it lifted above the vast green mantle of the jungle. Felix pressed his face to the window and felt an emptiness snatch at his chest. He would miss that simple, magical world and the tribe who'd accepted him as one of their own for the past two years.

Felix had finished his PhD in Biology, and then been funded by a pharmaceutical company for a project in the Amazon. He'd been there ever since, studying medicinal properties in hundreds of plants used by the inhabitants of the area to fight different diseases.

Felix reminisced as the aircraft gained altitude.
His arrival among the Umeni community deep in the jungle hadn't been easy. He had to communicate his intentions to the only member of the tribe who understood his language, and then he had to wait on the outskirts of the village while the tribe sat in a circle and discussed what to do.

When the meeting was over, he was invited to introduce himself to each member of the tribe.

"There are only twenty of us Umeni left in the entire world," explained the translator and speaker, "and we make all our important decisions as one."

The speaker went on to explain that every child born into the group was considered a gift from heaven. From birth they were immediately accepted as a member of the tribe. However, the acceptance of any human being from the world outside was something that had to be decided by the whole group. One new member to the community would change the lives of all of them, so all of them had to agree that the addition would be beneficial.

If anyone thought differently, even a child, the rest of the tribe would listen to his or her reasons, and the circle would discuss the issue again.

Felix sat waiting under a tree with a massive trunk. He watched the sun go down and rise again. Finally, the speaker came back to him with the good news: he'd been accepted. Ever since then, he'd been treated as yet another member of the Umeni tribe.

He was pulled out of his remembrances when a brown-skinned hostess handed him a tray with a carton of orange juice and a snack on it. The small meal reminded him of the many Umeni meetings that he had attended. It was a great memory, but his mind quickly returned to his current circumstances. He was sad to be leaving the friendly, natural world that he had become so used to.

Felix took two envelopes out of his rucksack. They'd been delivered with great difficulty to the secluded hamlet where he lived. The letter in the first envelope had broken the news of his father's sudden death to him. This was a surprise because Felix had not talked to his father since he married a woman nearly half his age.

The second letter was from Simon, his dad's accountant. Felix remembered him from when his parents were still married. Simon used to like making jokes, and always brought him antique toys for his collection.

Felix opened his letter, realising it must have been fifteen years since he'd last seen the accountant.

He took a sip of his orange juice and took a deep breath as he read through the letter, which was written in a cold, formal style, although it addressed him by his first name.

"*Dear Felix,*

You must be aware by now of your father's untimely death. Before I go on, let me express my sincere condolences.

I was informed by your university that you're living in a village with no telephone coverage. I find that admirable for someone in today's world. I am sending you this, then, by urgent post. I hope it reaches you before it's too late.

I know that your contact with your father in recent years has been sporadic at best. However, as his only heir, it is my obligation to explain his situation to you.

Your father was having financial problems towards the end of his life. He was forced to sell his house and mortgage the premises of his two bookstores, which are now in danger of closing down.

Your father's wife died a year ago. This means that your presence and authorization will be required to liquidate his business in as orderly a manner as possible, unless you prefer to do otherwise.

I hope to hear from you soon,

Yours sincerely,
Simon."

The happiest company in the world

Felix read over the letter a couple of times, feeling anxious as you do when confronting a possibly overwhelming task. Breathing in deeply, he took out one of the notebooks he'd bought in Manaos for his field notes. He hadn't touched the book yet, but he planned to use it to record the keys to his new challenge.

2.
Captain Flint

Felix took a rest at the hotel where he'd booked a room. It was strange to be living in a hotel in his home city, but he'd left his rented flat when leaving for the Amazon. A while later, he looked up the address of his dad's biggest bookstore, and set off out of the hotel.

The store was on the busiest street of the city centre. It should have been easy to find, but he hadn't been there for such a long time that he had to go back on his tracks several times before seeing the CAPTAIN FLINT sign. Only 8 of the 12 neon letters were working.

Felix hadn't spoken to his dad for a long time, and he realised sadly that he'd never asked him why he'd given the store that name.

He pushed open the heavy glass door and looked around. It felt like he was walking into a funeral home. There was absolute silence inside and not a single customer to be seen. The staff were moving lethargically around a space over a thousand metres squared.

Behind the cash register was a middle-aged woman sifting through a pile of delivery notes. Along the shelves, a

The happiest company in the world

skinny man was pushing a shopping cart with a list in his hand. He was taking some books off the shelves and putting others on, shuffling forward a few meters and then repeating the task.

Felix spotted a third shop assistant with his biologist's gaze and analysed him like some kind of exotic bird. He was a young man with long curly hair. He was sitting behind a circular counter signposted "Customer Service", fingering his Smartphone in total absorption.

Felix realised that nobody had a clue who he was, and that gave him an idea. He'd pretend to be a customer, and that would give him an inside look into how his dad's store was run.

He walked up to the curly-haired man's counter. It took a while for his presence to register, but finally the man raised his eyes from his screen and looked at him with a bored expression.

"Morning," said Felix.

The assistant raised his eyebrows questioningly and a little rudely, as if he'd been interrupted in the middle of something important.

"Excuse me – but before I ask anything else, I see the store is called Captain Flint. Who is that?"

"He's the parrot in *Treasure Island*," the man answered, irritated. "Anything else I can do for you?"

"Ah, of course – *Treasure Island*!" said Felix, playing the part of a trusting customer. "That was the first book my dad ever read. Amazing I could have forgotten that parrot's name... I'd really love to read the book again. Which publisher would you recommend?"

The assistant put his mobile phone away, and tapped unenthusiastically at his keyboard. His green eyes scanned a list on the screen.

Finally, he said, "I'm afraid we don't seem to have it in stock right now."

Felix was shocked. He glanced around. There must be at least ten thousand different books on sale in the store. Looking back at the assistant, he saw the man was poking at his smartphone again.

"How can a bookstore called Captain Flint not have a single copy of *Treasure Island?*" he asked.

The assistant shrugged.

3.
John Silver

After his short reconnaissance, Felix felt curious and decided he'd take a look at his dad's other shop.

As he headed to the outskirts of the city where the shop was, he thought how there was no need for him to ask why that one was called "John Silver". The name belonged to the pirate in *Treasure Island*, and his dad had always had a fascination for Stevenson's novel. He'd read Felix chapters from it every night until he was eight. His childhood memories of the wonderful story and its fascinating characters filled his eyes with tears. He came up onto the street and asked an elderly man walking his dog the way to the store. It turned out to be a small shop at the top of a steep street.

The pirate themed store was on the ground floor and was no larger than eighty square metres. It felt pleasantly cosy. The wooden floor creaked under Felix's feet as he stared at the chaos inside. He wondered how anyone ever found a single book in there.

Except for a couple of shelves, most of the books were heaped in disordered piles on large tables. Half a dozen clients wandered around the mountains of books like treasure hunters in search of hidden gold.

Jazz music played softly in the background.

Amazed that his dad's two bookstores could be so completely different, Felix searched around for a member of staff to talk to. The first person he saw was a plump man in a checked shirt who seemed to be taking an order on the phone.

Behind a tiny counter he saw a girl with plastic-rimmed glasses reading Nabakov's *Lolita*. She noticed him straight away, and marked her book with a pencil between its pages. Smiling openly, she spoke in a friendly tone of voice.

"Are you looking for anything special?"

"Yes, actually. *Treasure Island* is what I'm after. Could you take a look in your computer and see if you have any copies of it?"

"Um... none of our files are digitalized," she said, blushing. "We just use the computer to search for orders when we don't have them in stock."

Felix turned to look at the overflowing tables. "But how do you ever find anything in all this mess?" he asked.

"Well, it might seem impossible, but we know exactly where everything is. Your book is on the book by the window, in the second pile from there. It has a grey spine."

The happiest company in the world

Felix couldn't believe what he was hearing and went over to the table. The book was there, and he picked it up. A strange emotion went through him. The cover showed three pirates in a fighting stance. One of them was holding two single-shot pistols, the second one was brandishing a sable, and behind them, the third pirate was waving a black flag with a skull and crossbones on it.

By the time he got back to the counter with his find, the reader of *Lolita* had laid out a piece of tissue paper to wrap the book in.

Felix watched closely as her agile hands wrapped it up and sealed it, very appropriately, with a JOHN SILVER sticker.

He paid for the book, and was just about to leave when the shop assistant said, "By the way, I'm so sorry about your father."

Felix was stunned.

"How do you who I am?"

"You look just like him," she said shyly, "and you make the same kind of gestures."

KEY 1:
To make a happy company, we need to ask, "What can we do to make our business happier?"

Asking good questions is an essential step in discovering what can be improved and what each person can contribute to becoming an outstanding, satisfied member of staff.

Many companies make the same mistakes over and over, because they don't stop to think or allow their staff to ask whether they're doing their jobs in the best possible way.

Knowing how to ask is the first step in finding out what we need to implement to achieve new, hopeful results.

Anyone who gets bored at work, for instance, should ask themselves why, and what they can do to change that; or what other job could motivate them to give their best and feel fulfilled.

Don't feel afraid to ask these questions or look for the answers. A happy company and happy people ask themselves many things because they know it will make them happier.

STOP AND DECIDE TO BE HAPPY

The happiest company in the world

4.
Simon's report

After passing by both of the stores, Felix had lunch at a simple restaurant and sat for a while at the bar. He had to wait until four o'clock, when he was be meeting his dad's accountant and confidant to find out the state of the company's finances.

His work in the Amazon had been deeply satisfying to him as a biologist, but he had no savings to prop up any debts that the companies might have accumulated. He felt a gnawing concern.

To calm his nerves, he ordered a green tea and read the beginning of the book he'd bought at John Silver. He was surprised to find he couldn't remember a single word of the novel except for the song about the bottle of rum. This made him think that his dad must have read his own particular version aloud so Felix's young mind could understand.

He felt another stab of nostalgia, then paid and left for his appointment with Simon, whose office was on the main floor of an ancient office building.

The doorbell had a loud, harsh ring like they used to in his grandfather's time. The heavy wooden door opened seconds later, and Felix was taken back to the days of his childhood.

Simon looked almost exactly like he remembered. He'd been bald when Felix was a kid, and now what remained of this hair on his head was completely white; but his sharp expression and the twinkle in his eyes hadn't changed a bit.

He patted Felix on the back and led him into his office.

Felix felt like Simon was very happy to see him. He sat down in front of him as if the years hadn't gone by.
A globe and a fountain pen on its inkstand on the mahogany desk reminded him of an old doctor's office.

Felix was, in actual fact, about to find out about a dying patient's health.

Simon told him some of the details leading up to his dad's death.

Then he cleared his throat and began: "Things with the stores are desperate. We've been running at a loss for years, and we've been covering it with your father's assets. Our loan will give us just enough to pay salaries and rent until Christmas comes around, at a pinch – but it might be best to liquidate as soon as we can."

Felix gulped. He had years of experience in laboratory protocols, but he had no idea what you do with a failing bookstore. He felt overwhelmed. All the same, he didn't want to make any decisions until he could get a general view of the situation. To do that he would have to use the two things he

The happiest company in the world

did have; the scientific method and the Umeni's human knowledge.

He checked the calendar on his watch: Tuesday, October 14th. If their loan could get them through to Christmas, they would have only three short months to work with.

"I passed by both stores this morning," he said. "It seems like there's quite a lot going on at John Silver, but Captain Flint is completely empty."

"You're right. John Silver is tiny and not in a good spot, but we hardly have any losses there. Captain Flint is where most of our debts with our suppliers come from, even though that's the store that should work best because of its location. It's so hard to understand..."

Felix thought for a second. "Why do you think my dad named it after the parrot?" he asked.

"That's a secret, now!" said Simon with a mischievous grin. "Actually, the parrot in the story was named after Captain Jonathan Flint, the terrible pirate who buried his treasure. He's the reason behind the whole story."

"Perhaps my dad thought that bookstore would be a goldmine," Felix mused. "And I guess the other one's called John Silver because it's chaotic and bohemian, like a pirate tavern."

"Maybe... Your dad wasn't very talkative, as you know. Anyway, the thing is that we have to do something fast. The ship's sinking."

"Well, I need to have a talk with the crew before I decide which way we're going to sail."

The accountant coughed as he pulled a folder with dust from years back down from the shelf. He dropped it noisily on the desk. "Alright, let's do it" he said.

The happiest company in the world

5.
The Crew

Simon then told Felix about the staff at John Silver, his dad's first bookstore. The small ship was expertly sailed by a crew of just two, Austin and Elena.

"He does the most laborious, administrative work. He receives all the orders, does the returns, and runs the inventory of all that mess they claim has some kind of order in it."

"It does have a bohemian charm, but I'm sure things could be better organised," said Felix. "Tell me about Elena."

"Elena is an English major, and she's a walking archive. She can tell you who wrote and published almost any book you ask her for. She even knows when they're out of print and if you can get hold of them anywhere. She adores reading, but that used to annoy your dad a bit."

"Why?"

"Well, he didn't like her reading at work, even though she never minds doing a longer day if there are reading clubs to be organised."

"I call that leading by example," said Felix in Elena's defence. "I remember last time I was in Paris. I went to Shakespeare & Co., which is probably the world's most famous bookstore. When the assistants weren't needed by anyone, they'd sit there reading, and that gave all the customers a really interesting message."

"What kind of message?"

Simon seemed a little taken aback by Felix's arguments. After all, the last time he'd seen the boy he'd been playing with his toys.

"They're showing customers they love books, and so they must love their work. People will always go back, say, to a restaurant where the chef loves what he does. But we'll stay away from places where the staff act like they'll be gone tomorrow, or don't care."

"You sound like you're talking about Captain Flint," said the accountant.

"Everything is so organised in there, but you feel no emotion when you walk in. My visit was a real disappointment - but I didn't feel like that at John Silver."

"Yeah, I see what you mean... The thing is, I don't really understand why it's like that, because the staff have a lot of expertise. Gertrude, the cashier, has worked in bookstores for thirty years. She doesn't let a single detail go by; she manages everything... though I guess there hasn't been too much to manage lately." Simon stroked his chin and went on. "Maybe she's just lost all her spark because the business is failing."

The happiest company in the world

"What about that guy with the curly hair? He's supposed to be helping our customers, but they just seem to annoy him."

"That's Jonathan. I think he's coming out of a long depression. Any other company would've fired him by now. Your dad might have had a lot of faults, but he did look after his staff like they were his own children."

Simon halted, realising what he'd said, but Felix waved him on. He hadn't come back to civilization to pass judgement on his dad.

"There are two more stable employees at Captain Flint. The rest are just temporary staff we hire for the Christmas campaign. There's Peter, who manages stocks and stacks the shelves."

"Yeah, I saw him. Anyone else?"

"Nathalie. She's thirty, and she walks around the store answering questions in any of the sections. If you didn't see her, she must have been in the storeroom."

Felix didn't ask any more about her. He preferred to wait for his own impressions when he went back to the store. Before he made any decisions, he thought, he wanted to go back to Captain Flint and introduce himself as his father's son. He needed to find out what was going on in the crew's own words.

Simon pulled him out of his thoughts.

"You must be wanting to take a look at the accounts. Hold tight to your chair - they're a real mess..."

KEY 2:
A company's most valuable asset is the energy of the people who work there.

The quality of any company depends on the spirit of the people who work there. Businesses like 3M and Google set aside part of their workers' time for creative thought and inspiration for new projects.

Being aware of the creative potential of everyone who makes up a business, freelance workers included, will help you turn a simple workplace into the happiest company in the world.

Sharing reading material among your team is another way to bond and be inspired together. As Walt Disney said, "There is more treasure in books than in all the pirates' loot on Treasure Island."

TAKE CARE OF YOUR ENERGY

6.
The first meeting

The staff of Captain Flint were staring uneasily at Felix. All four of them were sitting on chairs placed in a circle at the back of the huge premises, in a space where no book presentations had been made for a long time.

The biologist in Felix was trying to work out at a single glance what each of their expressions revealed.

Jonathan seemed to be the most afraid. He'd recognised Felix immediately as the customer who'd unsuccessfully requested *Treasure Island*.

Gertrude was acting tensely self-sufficient. Behind her thick glasses, the expression in her eyes seemed to say, "I've been in this business for thirty years, and you might be the owner's son, but you haven't got a clue on how to run this place."

Peter was about fifty years old, and was hanging his head like an ox off to the slaughter.

Unlike him, Nathalie was shifting nervously and running her fingers through her hair, as if ready to defend her position. Her stocky body and determined gaze showed she was a strong woman.

The happiest company in the world

Before the meeting, Felix had pondered how different this circle was to the Umeni. The tribe had made every meeting a reason for celebration. The circle meant union to them, familiarity, laughs, giving ideas, strengthening ties, sharing...

Felix introduced himself briefly and thanked them for their attention. Then he decided to use a strategy the Umeni had taught him when trying to improve things in their village.

"Before we go on to the situation in general, I'd like each of you to tell me one thing that works and makes you happy, and one other thing that doesn't work here."

Peter's eyes widened and he tensed his skinny body like an antelope trying to struggle free of a trap. The first person to talk was Nathalie. She had a clear voice like a radio announcer.

"I work all around the shop, and I think the space is fantastic. But the sections are badly organized. So in the 'Novels' section, say, if the customer doesn't know where the writer is from, it's impossible for them to find the book without asking for help, because all the novels are ordered by the language they were written in. That doesn't make any sense."

"We can change that together," said Felix. "What about you, Jonathan? What do you think?"

The young, curly-haired man gulped, then said, "Well, my counter is in the middle of the bookstore. The computer program we use for stock control is fast and effective. But the thing that hasn't been working well is... me. I have to admit I'm not at my best right now."

His three colleagues were amazed at his show of sincerity.

Felix didn't hesitate to respond. "There are days when I don't work well, either; but we're going to create the right circumstances so that we can change that."

"You mean outside the store?" asked Jonathan, feeling like dismissal was imminent.

"This, people, is Captain Flint. It's our ship. What happens in other seas is none of my business."

The meeting wasn't going quite as they expected. Peter felt encouraged and said, "I take my work really seriously, but it's boring pushing a trolley around and reading a list for hours on end."

"Don't worry. We'll find ways to solve things. This isn't an assembly line, is it. We sell books – that is, we sell the authors' spirit. We have to know how to get that across if we want the customers to come."

"You've taken the words out of my mouth, Felix," said Gertrude dryly. "The good thing about my work is that I have everything completely up to date. The bad thing is, there are no customers."

"And what do you plan to do to change that?"

The happiest company in the world

The cashier was surprised. Before she could come up with any excuses, Felix went on. "I have some new orders for you, crew. From now on, everything that happens in this store depends on you. We've taken command, and we're responsible for where the ship sails from now on. Never again will we blame anything external for what goes on inside here."

"But there's a crisis in the book sector," said Peter. "Statistics say less and less people are buying books."

"People are what I care about, not statistics," said Felix. "Captian Flint can succeed if we're passionate about what we do and give our customers something unique. The crisis needn't come into it."

Felix had declared his principles. And he realised that without planning to, he'd just saved the bookstore's life. At least for now.

7.
The binary test

Back in his hotel room, Felix sat down at the small desk with a sheet of white paper and a pen in front of him. He was about to analyse what he'd seen at the two stores, and his meeting at Captain Flint, in the simplest, most scientific way he could.

Early on in his stay in the Amazon, he'd been amazed by how the Umeni divided everything that affected the tribe into two categories: IT MAKES US HAPPY, or IT DOESN'T MAKE US HAPPY. Attitudes and changes that made them happy were encouraged, while the things that made them unhappy were eradicated or substituted for others that could contribute to the common good. It was as simple as that. Now, Felix was wondering whether he'd be able to use the binary test on his dad's failing enterprise.

He set to his task straight away. On one side of the page, he wrote down the name of the bigger store, and then what didn't work and what did.

CAPTAIN FLINT

NO (doesn't make us happy):

- NO customers.
- NO good customer service.

The happiest company in the world

- NO predefined company values.
- NO staff motivation
- NO innovation (everything always done the same way, even if it doesn't work).
- NO dynamism.
- NO future aims.

Final note: We often leave our passion at home.
YES (makes us happy):
- STOCK is well sorted and managed.
- STOCK is varied for all clients (though no copies of *Treasure Island*).
- SPACE is large (customers can walk comfortably around 1000m2).
- STAFF are well-trained (skills not always fully used).

Felix then used the same test on the small bookstore.

JOHN SILVER

NO (doesn't make us happy):

- NOT enough space for everything we stock.
- NO order on the shelves (chaotic placement of books so that customers can't find what they're looking for without help).
- NO archive to search for customer requests.

YES (makes us happy):

- STAFF are skilled (& seem to like the store)
- GOOD customer service.
- PASSION transmitted by 2 staff (who seem to love their jobs).
- STAFF preach by example (reading).
- KNOWLEDGE of what we sell (Elena seems to know every edition of every book on the market).
- DYNAMISM (Reading group twice monthly in the back half of the store).

That done, Felix looked up from his task and out of the window. The sky had clouded over and it looked like it was

The happiest company in the world

going to rain. He didn't want to have to buy an umbrella, so he left the hotel straight away for John Silver. He was going to put his analysis to use.

8.
Balancing out

On his way to the pirate bookstore, Felix stopped at a cake shop a little way up the same steep, narrow street. He ordered a dozen small croissants and three orange juices to take away.

By the time he got to John Silver, improvised tea in hand, it was near closing time. There were still several customers browsing through the piles on the tables.

Felix left his brown bag on a windowsill and spent a couple of minutes searching through the books for a hidden treasure.

Ella Fitzgerald was playing in the background, and it gave the place a pleasant, warm atmosphere.

Once Austin and Elena had said goodbye to the last customers, all of whom left with a book or two, Felix himself locked the door behind them.

"There's so much going on here," he said. "Now, let's sit down and have a quick something to eat, and I'll tell you about this test I've done on the store."

Elena adjusted her glasses and looked at him curiously. Meanwhile, Austin fetched the three folding chairs they used for the reading clubs. He put them next to the window around a small table for the croissants and juices.

The happiest company in the world

Felix sat down with the two assistants and took a sip of his juice.

"Before I begin, I'd like to say thanks to both of you for the great work you're doing. With all its inconveniences, this store has a soul, and you can see all the customers feel at home here."

"They do, don't they," smiled Elena. "Some of them spend even more time here than they do in their own homes."

Austin gave her a mischievous glance and stroked his beard. Felix guessed they both knew exactly who they were talking about.

"There are a lot of values here that we should foster. But I'm going to begin with the things that *don't* work. There aren't many of them. But for instance, when you walk in you feel like there isn't enough space to display all the books."

"We like to have all our variety at hand, right here," argued Austin. "And our customers actually seem to like browsing through the piles on the tables. Even if they're overflowing, I still put out anything new that comes in."

"Is there an order, or some kind of theme to each table?" asked Felix.

"Well, each table supposedly has a theme: novels, essay, guidebooks, children's books, and so on... But in practice, the customers are always putting things back in the wrong place."

"If we didn't know each book like shepherds know their sheep," added Elena, "there's no way we'd be able to find them again."

Felix took a bite out of a croissant and thought for a moment.

"All this chaos has its appeal. It makes the place sort of romantic. But I bet you waste a lot of time because of it. Every time a customer asks for a book it must be like searching for a star in the sky." Felix stroked his chin. "What happens when two or three people ask for a book at the same time?"

"They have to wait a little while," said Elena, "but we're fast."

"I'm sure you are. But don't you think it'd be a lot more practical if they could find the books themselves? Then you could concentrate on what you do best, which is making good recommendations."

Felix stood up as he pieced together all his thoughts.

"We need to foster everything that's good here, which is a lot. But we're also going to look for a more rational way to stack the books and put in some extra shelves. We'll put together a database so that everyone who comes in can look for what they want. It'll be online so that customers can order books from home, buy the digital version with a podcast review by us, or come and look for it and hear first hand what the book is like."

The happiest company in the world

"Great idea!" said Austin, folding up his chair. "Let's start right now, shall we?"

"No," said Felix, "That won't be necessary. Tomorrow will be both of your last day at John Silver."

KEY 3:
Doing things simply will help your company to be happy.

Investing your energy in what you do best, and not letting yourself be waylaid by secondary issues, are ways to make sure that "less is more". This is a good motto for any company or any personal project.

Getting rid of bureaucracy and hierarchies, for instance, is a way to simplify the direction of a company. That way, everyone can give the best of themselves without having to go through intermediaries or filters. Instead of a boss, make a "happiness manager".

In the happiest company in the world, then, we don't speak of middle management, but of people rowing together, each of them adding the best of their ideas and talent. If what we want to achieve is hard to explain or we can't find a straightforward way to do so, it might not be the best way forward. Simplicity is beautiful, and beauty makes us happy.

In happy companies, technology works for us, and frees us up to choose the simplest way to make decisions.

SIMPLIFY

9.
Breaking the news

The next day was Friday, and Felix went down to Captain Flint to balance things out on the other side. He found the staff fully occupied, though it was early in the morning and no customers had come in yet.

Armed with a bag of croissants and a tray with five coffees from a café along the way, Felix and Nathalie set up a large table in the same place as the day before.

When all the staff were seated, Felix laid out the conclusions from his binary test.

"Let me start with the good things. There are a lot of different books in here – although one important one is missing – and the customers can walk around comfortably." He paused. "And all of you are well-trained and good enough at what you do to help out even the most demanding customers."

Jonathan's shoulders tensed. He knew his first encounter with his boss hadn't been the best example of fine customer service, even though he hadn't known who he was.

"How about the bad things?" said Gertrude drily. "That's what you're here for, isn't it?"

"Actually, I wanted to speak about both good and bad," said Felix, smiling. "The good things will always speak for themselves, though. All you have to do is foster them and strengthen them. But with the things that *don't work*, I'll lay them out for you so that you can come up with some solutions yourselves."

Peter shrunk in his chair. The old bosses' son looked like he was going to give things at Captain Flint a good shaking up.

"I don't see any clear company values here," began Felix. "What distinguishes you from your competitors? What makes you, the staff, stand out? Why would anyone choose to come here instead of ordering online and having books delivered to their homes?"

Nobody knew what to answer.

Felix went on enthusiastically.

"When we have the answers to those questions, we'll go from being an empty wasteland to a space where customers feel at home and want to come back to."

He took a sip of his coffee, which was cold by now, and went on.

"The thing is, this store seems devoid of ideas – except for the ones in the books, of course. You walk through the place and everything always looks exactly the same."

"The books change," interjected Nathalie, "but we could also change around the sections we put them in."

The happiest company in the world

"We could do that, but I'm thinking of a different kind of innovation." Felix paused thoughtfully. "I'd like people who come into Captain Flint to have the feeling that there are things going on here."

"You mean promotions and discounts?" asked Gertrude.

"Yes, that's one possibility – but what I mean is, we need things that involve you as the staff. Customers ought to feel they're walking into a temple of books where they're going to feel deep emotions and find treasures, to honour the name of the store."

"We haven't done any book presentations for ages," said Jonathan, "because only a few people ever came. But we could try again and see if they worked better."

"If nobody came, we need to ask what could have been done better. Or, thinking positively, what could be improved to make people want to come."

There was a silence, and then Gertrude spoke.

"As you can see, we're not very used to taking the initiative. But if you suggest all the changes we have to make, we'll bring them in in no time."

"There'll be changes, and we'll work out what they're going to be together. But not all of you will have the chance to bring them in." It was time for him to break the news. "Actually, as of tomorrow, two of you won't be coming back to Captain Flint."

10.
A place for everyone

The autumn was turning out to be more like an extended summer. Felix had spent his weekend strolling around a park near his hotel with his notebook. Big changes were coming, and he wanted to stay on top of every detail. They only had two months to get the stores back on their feet. If sales didn't start growing, and if their Christmas campaign didn't have the effect they needed, they wouldn't be able to pay back their loan and the bank would freeze their liquidity.

Felix had chosen to change the *NOs* on his list by making a risky change: the two talented employees at John Silver would change over to Captain Flint, which was well-located and big enough to have enormous business potential; and two of the staff there would move over to the "pirate store" where the customers were all established and all that was needed was a little order.

Felix had learned from the Umeni that everyone can shine if they're given a place to do so. Just as different things will grow better in their own soil, each person has his or her place.

To his surprise, neither of the staff at John Silver showed any reluctance to what he proposed. In actual fact, the idea seemed to motivate them.

"At last we can get out of this cave!" said Elena happily. "I think I've read every single book I care to read here. There are twenty times the number at Captain Flint."

"But don't you feel sad to leave this place?"

"Not at all," replied Austin. "It'll be a challenge for us to build up our clientele at a place where most people are just passing by."

"We'll have to put our heads to work," smiled Elena.

The changes weren't so well received at Captain Flint. Nobody understood why two of the employees there, Jonathan and Gertrude, would be going over to John Silver. And they found it even harder to understand why the two remaining staff, Peter and Nathalie, would be given new positions.

"You've been doing the same old stuff for too long," Felix explained patiently. "Einstein used to say that we can't get different results by always doing things the same way."

"I understand that Gertrude would be the best person to get things in order at John Silver," said Nathalie, not caring to hide her disgust, "and that the bohemian atmosphere there might put some life back into Jonathan – after all, he was

The happiest company in the world

feeling a bit lonely here; but I'd have preferred to stay just where I was, not at the customer service counter."

"But you're the best one here for this position," said Felix. "You know every inch of the store, and you can easily help people to find what they're looking for. You don't have to sit there the whole day – you can always take them to the shelves yourself if there's no-one waiting. That'd give them a different kind of experience to what they get at the moment, wouldn't it?"

Nathalie nodded gently, like he was managing to persuade her. Felix went on.

"And Peter has been pushing the trolley around for too many years now. It'll be good for him to be able to sit down at the cash register and take care of the paperwork when he's not dealing with the customers. He's got a gentle manner, too, and customers will feel good leaving the store just after speaking to him. Remember, what we want is for them to come back."

Peter responded with a nervous smile. But there was also a shine in his eyes. Taking on a new responsibility made him feel like he was beginning again.

And that was a good thing.

KEY 4:

The mission of a happy company is to get the people who belong to it to do what they do best.

All of us are good at something, and we'll give the best of ourselves when we're able to work at what we can shine in and feel fulfilled doing.

Apathy and lack of identification with your job can transform into enthusiasm and exceptional performance when people have the chance to do the right job.

When something or someone isn't working well, stop to think if they're really doing the right job for them and their personal strengths.

The task of a company – and that of every person in it – is to discover how each member of it can be most useful to others.

DO WHAT YOU DO BEST

11.
A "Wow" experience

Felix witnessed some amusing scenes at the small John Silver store during the first few days of the changeover. He spent quite a lot of his time there, and Simon often came along.

Sitting in a reading corner that Gertrude had set up so that they could keep out of the customers' way, Simon observed the changes with the curiosity of someone watching a sociological experiment.

"I thought this was going to be a disaster, but I guess I'm wrong. Everything seems to have changed, except for the essentials..."

"Gertrude moved things around a bit at the back, but she made sure the place lost none of its charm," explained Felix. "She's really meticulous, so any book that gets put back in the wrong place doesn't stay there for long. And she's building the database herself so that we know exactly what's in here."

"Jonathan seems a lot happier, too."

Both of them looked up at what had previously been Elena's desk. The curly-haired young man was patiently listening to a discussion between two elderly professors on which was the best translation of *Ulysses* on the market.

Days later, Simon and Felix, heir to the two stores, made a visit to the newly renovated Captain Flint to see how the latest additions to the crew were faring.

The first thing they noticed were backlit photographic images announcing each different section. "Foreign Novels" was advertised with a large portrait of Ernest Hemingway, surrounded by cats. In the "Science" section was Einstein on a bicycle. Children's and young adult's literature was presided by a charming photo of Astrid Lindgren, the maker of *Pippi Langstrump,* with the actress who'd played the part of the character and Mr. Nilsson, her inseparable monkey.

"Looks like this graveyard is coming alive at last!" commented Simon admiringly. "And it's not just the photos. There are customers here!"

"Yes, they're starting to come in," said Felix happily, "but I reckon this is only the beginning."

It was afternoon, and there were about twelve people wandering around the different sections, where Elena was answering their questions. At the customer service counter, Nathalie was helping out a granddad looking for a book on quantum physics for his grandchildren.

"Try *The Door with Three Locks* by Sonia Fernández-Vidal," she suggested.

The happiest company in the world

A short queue of customers were being attended to by Peter at the till, and Austin was pushing his trolley around each section making sure all the new arrivals were on the shelves.

"There's something I want to show you," said Felix, beckoning Simon over to a new corner set up for presentations and reading clubs.

Simon walked through a pair of red curtains. Behind them was a comfortable space, with forty chairs and a large white panel with the word "Wow!" on it.

Wow!

"What on Earth does that mean?" asked the accountant.

"It sums up exactly what we want people to feel when they walk in here. We aren't just selling books; we're also selling a passion for reading. A "Wow!" experience.

12.
Green for happiness

Before Felix came across his first big problem in his new adventure, he decided to bring in a novelty. Like others, it was inspired by the Umeni.

In the village where he'd spent his two years there was an ancient ritual that he'd found remarkable ever since he first observed it.

Everyone was given three bracelets to wear as soon as they were born, and on ritual days the number went up to ten. Any member of the tribe would wear all three bracelets proudly if they felt happy. When they didn't feel quite so good, they would take one of them off and wear two. When the number went down to one, it meant the person was feeling very down at heart or having serious problems.

Whenever this happened, the tribe would go and see the sad member and make a circle to help him or her.

Jonathan turned out to be a computer wizard, and had helped Felix install the equivalent to the ritual on each of their computers.

The happiest company in the world

Every morning, when they turned them on, a sentence appeared:

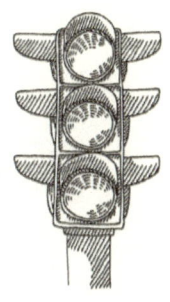

"HOW ARE YOU TODAY?"

NOT WELL

NOT TOO BAD

GREAT!

At first, the traffic light had been more of a surprise than anything else, but after a week it had become a ritual that brought out good feeling and jokes from the staff at both stores.

From his small office in the storeroom of Captain Flint, the biologist took a look at his staff's moods once a day before he went over the accounts, orders and returns.

One morning, just a month before Christmas, four of them had come to work feeling GREEN, but Gertrude had chosen amber. She'd gotten out of bed with lumbago and was waiting for an appointment with her osteopath.

Then in the third week of November, a red light appeared for the first time. It was Jonathan.

Felix called John Silver a couple of times, but the phone was engaged as usual. The store's most faithful customers normally made their orders by phone.

He felt uneasy and decided to take the underground over to the store and find out what was wrong.

He found Jonathan slumped over his counter, with Gertrude watching him sideways as she stacked the books on the tables.

"Is something wrong?" Felix asked him in a low voice, putting his hand on his shoulder. "Have you and Gertrude been arguing about something?"

"No, not at all... She's even kinder to me than my favourite aunt."

"Are things not going well for you at home? If you like, I can take over from here and you can go and sort them out."

"No, it's not that... it's... me, Felix. I need to leave this job."

13.
A meeting for happiness

That night, Felix invited the team to a pizza restaurant in the city centre for a *happiness meeting*. He'd decided he'd do one every month as of January to keep in touch with how the crew were feeling, but Jonathan's news was out of the ordinary and he felt he should call a special one right away.

He thanked everyone for agreeing to forsake dinner in the privacy of their homes just so they could hear out Jonathan, who began:

"Now that I'm at John Silver, where there's a really great atmosphere, I've realised that this job is just not right for me. I don't really like it. I used to be able to blame the store for that – how big and empty it was; but here... Now I realise this just isn't my place. I'd love to be a customer here, but I shouldn't be working here."

"What could we do to make you feel better?" asked Felix, as he topped up their glasses with a Lambrusco rosé.

"If you find it stressful dealing with the public I can always hand over my position to you," suggested Austin. "And you can stroll around pushing the trolley. How about that?"

"Maybe he's sick of people asking him questions the whole time," interjected Peter. "If you feel like you should be sitting behind the register, and everyone thinks it's okay, you can take my place. I'd be fine anywhere I can feel useful, even if I have to go back to the trolley."

Jonathan looked around at all of them, visibly moved. He shrugged, not knowing how to explain what was troubling him.

Finally, he took a sip of his Lambrusco and said,

"Actually, what I really need is for all of you to help me leave. All this kindness is just making it harder for me."

His statement threw cold water on the group's enthusiasm. Jonathan realised he might have hurt their feelings, so he carried on. "I feel privileged to have worked with people like you, who do a much better job than I do." A knot seemed to form in his throat. "If it were only about the team, I'd stay here forever, but I've realised working with books is just not my thing, and it makes me feel frustrated. I'm convinced there are people out there who can do the job a thousand times better than me."

"Don't worry about others," Felix said. "Worry about yourself. What is it that makes you think you're not good at this?"

"I don't know all that many books. In fact, I think I've only read the same old stuff as everyone else."

The happiest company in the world

"What's so bad about that?" said Elena. "You could be our mainstream advisor!"

Jonathan sighed.

"Look, let's not keep on at him," said Felix. "I just want to ask you one more question, Jonathan. Right now, at this moment in your life, what do you think could make you happy?"

"Um..." Jonathan hesitated. "I think it would be something creative I could do on my own, but which could be useful to a lot of people... Do you think I can find something like that?"

Felix smiled gently. "I'm quite sure you can," he said.

14.
First values meeting

Felix posted adverts in several different literary webs to cover Jonathan's vacancy. Then one day, he organised a breakfast to discuss something he considered vital. All of the staff at both stores were there, and Simon came too.

Before they hired anyone new, it was essential they all got together to define the company's values.

Both stores opened at half past ten, and the meeting took place at a tearoom half way between them.

"When I was living in a tribe in the Amazon jungle," explained Felix, "all important decisions were made together, especially concerning anything that would affect the whole tribe. And what could be more important than a new sailor coming on board a ship like Captain Flint?"

"Does that mean we're going to have to give our opinions on the candidates?" asked Gertrude.

"It means more than that! It means you'll play an active part in selecting them. You're going to have to spend all day with whoever we hire, and they can improve everyone's time at work or make it worse. The Umeni divide everything into two very definite categories: things that add and things that take away." Felix opened his hands to include everyone.

The happiest company in the world

"The same thing will happen with whomever we hire here. If we make a good choice, we'll add value to our day and it'll be more pleasant and productive. But if we make a mistake, then we'll just be adding one more problem to our list. That's why I want everyone to be involved in this." He paused. "But before we begin, we really need to define the values behind our work at the stores. If we're not sure what they are, we won't be able to choose the right person."

He was answered by an expectant silence, which was broken by Austin, who stroked his chin and said, "Do you mean our own personal values? Or the values we want the store to communicate?"

"It'll be a mixture of the two. I'm going to ask you all a question now. What do you all value about working at a bookshop?"

"Well, I love being surrounded by books, of course," said Elena, "and having the chance to recommend our customers the best ones. I like knowing they trust us to give them books that will change their lives."

Felix raised his hand enthusiastically to contribute to her point.

"I think you've just mentioned two really interesting values, Elena. The first one would be passion for our product – books. Only if you love what you do can you sell it honestly. And the second, our vocation to help and inspire our customers."

"That's what creates addiction, in the good sense of the word," said Peter. "When customers feel they're being treated well, they'll come back of their own accord."

"That's right, because we like repeating nice experiences, don't we," said Felix. "That's how we create fidelity between a client and a brand, that is, the bookshops we're trying to bring back to life. Didn't someone once say that happiness is repeating?"

"That was Milan Kundera," smiled Elena.

"Well then, we have a basic leitmotif for our company: making our customers happy."

"To get them to come back," added Gertrude.

"That's not the only reason, remember – we don't just want them to come back. We also want to do our job well. Because there's an added reason to make our customers happy that has nothing to do with results - at least not financial results."

The five members of staff and the accountant all stared curiously at him as a waiter served them tea and biscuits.

"If we make them happy, we'll also be happy ourselves. Our self-esteem and the meaning of our lives are closely bound to how useful we feel to others. If we manage to get everyone who comes in here to leave feeling satisfied

The happiest company in the world

and well looked after, our traffic lights will always be on green."

"Sounds more like an NGO than a bookshop," joked Austin.

"Well, our final aim is an ambitious one, but it's wonderful. That's why it's worth aspiring to."

"What is it, then?" asked Nathalie, who was looking a little uncomfortable.

"In a nutshell our objective is: to be the happiest company in the world."

15.
A great idea

The day after the meeting, while Felix was in the bank discussing the terms of the loan with them, his phone alerted him that a message had come in.

ELENA
I've just had what might be a really good idea.
Got a moment today?

Felix had been waiting for his turn, and now the bank clerk was picking up a phone call and ignoring him. He checked his watch. It was nearly half past one. He tapped a message back.

FELIX
How about lunch at the Japanese restaurant next to Captain Flint?

ELENA
Great!
I'll close shop for lunch and see you there.

The happiest company in the world

Felix got to the small restaurant just before two. There were always one or two tables occupied by Japanese people, which was always a good sign.

He ordered *edamame*, soy beans that were eaten like peanuts, and a cold beer as he thought back over the main ideas that had come up at the values meeting. He jotted them down in his notebook:

CAPTAIN FLINT & JOHN SILVER: OUR VALUES

1. We love books.
2. We like finding treasure & sharing it with others.
3. We create happy moments.

Felix stopped then. Elena was coming through the door holding a bag full of books, smiling from ear to ear. For the first time since he'd embarked on the crazy adventure, the biologist realised how attractive he found her.

"What's that you're writing?" she asked him, giving him the customary kiss on both cheeks.

"I'm making a list of the values we came up with at the meeting yesterday."

"I think I have another one for you," she said, cradling her chin in her hands. "Now that we're starting to build up some regular customers at the main store, I've realised what's missing there."

"What is it?"

"Product involvement, as a marketing expert might say. Anyone would be horrified to see an Apple employee using any old PC, wouldn't they? How can we get through to our customers if we don't set an example?"

"When you were working at John Silver you always had your nose in a book, didn't you. Is that what you mean? That Captain Flint staff should always be reading so that the customers understand what it is you're selling?" joked Felix.

"Actually, what I'm thinking about is a bit more sophisticated than that," she grinned. "I thought about how we could share the books we enjoyed discovering for ourselves, and I remembered the "book people" in *Farenheit 451*."

"Um, I haven't read that myself," he said, embarrassed.

"It's a dystopia about a society where reading has been banned, and the firemen have to burn all the books. So to prevent losing all the great stories, there's a secret society who memorize the books and read them out to others. Each person remembers one book," she explained excitedly. "So

The happiest company in the world

one person would be *Don Quixote,* say, and another one *A Hundred Years of Solitude,* and so on."

"Okay, so what's your idea then...?" asked Felix curiously as the waiter handed them the menu.

"I wasn't thinking of anything gargantuan like having to learn entire books by memory, don't worry. I just thought of a nice detail that customers might notice and like."

Felix rested his fingertips together, intrigued.

"Each time one of us reads a book, what we could do is write down a sentence we really like and have a t-shirt printed with it. There are plenty of digital printing companies that could run them off in a couple of minutes."

Felix was interested. "What effect do you think it'd have on the public?"

"Well, they all like reading, so they'd be bound to notice and would most likely ask, "Hey, where did you get that sentence?" And the assistant could say, "So and so in such and such a book said it. It's a wonderful book – why don't you take a look at it."

"Great stuff," said Felix, and then jotted down another point in his list.

We adore great ideas.

16.
Recruitment begins

On Friday morning, Simon had called Felix to his office to find out if he'd need any help in drawing up the contract for the new member of staff at John Silver. Gertrude was alone at the store, and he was stepping in until they found someone new.

"We still haven't found anyone," he admitted.

"What? With all those people out there looking for work, how can it be so hard?"

"You're right," said Felix. "There are plenty of people looking for work. The thing is, it's not that easy to find the right one. It's a bit like a scientific procedure, like a biologist following a long protocol in a lab."

"Don't you think a recruitment agency might do a better job?" asked Simon innocently.

"Would they know our values?"

The accountant was thrown off track by Felix's answer. Slowly, he spun the globe on his desk.

"If you don't want to use an agency, then I guess you'll have to select your candidates yourself."

The happiest company in the world

"Actually," said Felix, "we'll all be doing it together. As they come in we'll take a good look at who they are and start filtering them according to our values."

"What exactly are you looking for?" Simon asked with real curiosity.

"It'll probably be faster if I tell you what we're *not* looking for. We've discarded any C.V.s that have been sent mechanically, without a personalised letter of presentation. We also ignore any that show that the person knows nothing about the company."

"Seems pretty logical so far. And then what do you look for in the C.V.? After all, all you need is someone to help the customers."

"Ah, but there's a magic to that job, we think, and so we don't want just anyone to do it," said Felix determinedly. "We look for extraordinary things in the C.V.s -and I'm not talking about people's schoolmarks here. People who've worked on cooperative projects, say, or thought up something that never existed before... We want people who want to do things. Our ad for the position is quite straightforward on that: PASSIONATE ASSISTANT REQUIRED."

"Very well," said Simon, folding his hands together and leaning back in his chair. "So how many C.V.s have grabbed your attention out of all that have come in since you put out the advert?"

"We've selected around fifteen of them. Look, here's one I like..."

Felix opened his briefcase and took out a photograph. A young, skinny man was standing in a room whose walls were lined with rows and rows of books.

"His name's Ian, and he sent us this photo of his room. You can see straight away that books are his life. If only for that, it seems like a good idea to get in touch with him."

"So you'll be interviewing fifteen people at the store?"

"No, not quite yet. I don't want to waste their time and money on transport. So we'll call them up first. Four questions will be enough to see whether they can go through to the second stage."

"Four questions?" asked Simon. "What are they?"

"You'll see now. Has your phone got hands-free? I'm going to give that guy who sleeps in his piles of books a call."

17.
The phone interview

Simon turned on hands-free and waited, itching with curiosity, for Felix to begin his conversation with the young man in the photo. He answered his phone as soon as it rang.

"I'm the manager of the bookshop where you sent your job application," said Felix by way of an introduction. "Before I go on, I'd like to thank you for the time you spent emailing us with your CV and photo. You've got a lot of books, haven't you?"

"Yeah," said Ian, chuckling. "Too many, my mum says."

"You can never have too many books... Well, Ian, as this is our first call, I'm only going to ask you four questions. Answer as freely as you like, alright?"

"I'll do that."

"What are you aiming for, professionally?"

Simon's eyes widened. That wasn't an easy question.

"I aim to work at what I enjoy doing," said Ian without hesitation. "And what I like best in the world is reading, so I can't think of a better place to work than a bookshop. I don't aspire to anything more."

"Great. My second question might surprise you, but just answer it honestly, okay? What can you do really well?"

"What do you mean, exactly?" asked Ian, a little hesitantly. "At work, or in my private life?"

"I mean, in general, what are you good at?"

"Well, I'm good at reading, discovering new books and recommending them to the right people. I am not usually wrong, because I'm aware that what I like might be absolutely awful for someone else."

Simon gave the thumbs up sign, but Felix waved his hand as if to say, "I'm not so sure..." Ian's answer was so perfect it was hard to believe he was really sincere.

"My third question is, what kind of work aren't you much good at?"

"Umm... I hate adding and subtracting, anything with figures. I'm terrible at it. I'd never have applied for a job as a cashier, because nothing would ever add up at the end of the day."

"Wonderful, Ian. Thanks for being so clear. Anyway, now for my last question..."

"Go ahead."

"Could you give me your last bosses' contact details so I could ask for a reference?"

The question seemed to throw Ian a little off balance.

The happiest company in the world

"My last job was as a copyrighter for a publisher who shut down last month. I promise it wasn't my fault..."

Felix responded with a gentle laugh, and asked, "Could you give me your bosses' telephone number?"

Ian dictated the editor-in-chief's number down the line. "Are you going to call him up right now?" he asked.

"I might. But just tell me one thing – what do you think he'd say about you?"

"What?" asked Ian, more and more disconcerted.

"Just imagine you're him, and I ask you for a reference. What would you say to me about yourself?"

"Well, I don't want to blow my own trumpet, but all of it would be good, I reckon. The editor-in-chief always had a high opinion of me."

"That's all I wanted to know, Ian," said Felix. "I'll let you know if we'll be able to meet personally. Thanks again for your time."

18.
Virtuous circle

November was drawing to a close. Felix decided to take a break from his search for the new member of his team.

The Umeni had taught him a saying: "You can't enjoy the night until you say goodbye to the day." Jonathan had popped into his mind several times that day. His contract was over, and he'd been paid what he was owed after his resignation, but Felix wondered how he was feeling, and if he'd managed to find a new direction in his life.

The Umeni also advised, "Pay attention to your heart; it sees further than your eyes." Felix realised it was time he sent Jonathan a message and asked to see him.

His ex-employee was surprised when he got in touch, but they arranged to meet and take a walk in the biggest park in the city.

As they strolled along the shore of a large pond, Felix told Jonathan that he simply wanted to see him to find out how he was doing, and asked if he could help with anything at all. Jonathan gave a sigh of relief.

"I thought you were about to ask me back to work for the Christmas campaign. It starts in three weeks, doesn't it?"

The happiest company in the world

"I'd never do that, Jonathan. You realised the job wasn't for you, and I just wanted to know if you've found a new direction in your life."

"Not really... in fact, I sometimes wonder if everyone actually has a passion," Jonathan mused. "Maybe there are guys like me who just never find what they like doing."

"That's impossible! If you search hard enough, you'll find what makes your life meaningful. I think it was Viktor Frankl who said, "If you don't know what your mission in life is, you have one now: finding it."

Jonathan smiled shyly. He liked the idea. At the same time, he found it strange to be talking about something like that on a Saturday afternoon with his ex boss.

Felix insisted. "The first step towards being happy is enjoying every little thing you do. When you find something you like, you do it a lot better and get much better results. That gives you confidence and helps you as a person, in your love life, for instance. If you feel happy and satisfied, your partner will feel it too, and will fill you with positive energy, which will make you happier, and in turn you'll get even better results. It's a virtuous circle, you see? Anyway, I just wanted to say that everything good we put into our lives comes back in some way."

"And everything bad, too," said Jonathan ironically. "I reckon I've spent the best part of my life feeding into a circuit of negative thinking. That's why I ended up getting depressed."

"But as soon as you realise that it might be enough to change something inside you, and change everything, see? And by the way, isn't there anything you remember from the bookshop that makes you feel good?"

Jonathan ran his fingers through his hair and said, "Well... There were the other staff... and I also had a fun time designing those traffic lights for everyone, although I didn't quite finish the whole idea. I think something else should have come up on the screen before you had to choose your mood for the day."

"Why don't you do that for us, and we'll pay you by the hour?" suggested Felix, who suddenly remembered something that had come up at the last meeting. "There's something else, too – our website isn't at all inviting, and nor is it user-friendly. It's a simple, static page with just a bit of information on it. What about redesigning it for us?"

Jonathan's eyes sparkled at the challenge. "Why not? That page is awful, it really is."

KEY 5:
Continuous personal and professional learning and growth are the backbone of a happy company.

The world never stops changing, and if we don't change with it we can no longer adapt and be happy in the world we live in. Our work needs to be a space for continuous training, where new tasks take the place of monotony. Even if we always have to do the same things, the way we approach them – whether we do so creatively and adaptively, or with the same inertia as ever – will mean the difference between a tedious job and a space for growth.

Innovation, and paying attention to the unexpected, are fundamental values for a happy company.

Every happy company should give its team new opportunities to learn and share their knowledge with others.

LEARN EVERY DAY

19.
Green for happiness (II)

The following Monday, each one of the staff turned on their computers and saw a new message waiting for them.

```
GOOD MORNING!
"Write your mistakes in the sand, so
that the waves of your achievements will
erase them."
(Anonymous).

How are you today? —>
```

To answer the question, they had to click on a link which opened a small form:

How are you today?
o   Bright Green
o   Green
o   Amber
o   Red

The happiest company in the world

Would you like to say why?
- o   Personal reasons
- o   Professional reasons

Any comments? Here's your space:
_____

SEND

With Jonathan's new system, there were four different moods and two areas in their lives to choose from. The team members could write messages to explain why they chose that colour, and each morning's results would be sent to a database which showed weekly, monthly and yearly graphs of the crews' emotions. This was really a great addition.

"Our first candidate for Captain Flint will be coming in today," said Felix to the staff. "He's that guy in the photo I showed you."

"The book nerd," smiled Elena.

"Right. Ian will be in in half an hour, so get ready to meet him."

"Are we going to have to interview him?" asked Peter.

"No, not exactly. It'd be really stressful for four people - five, that is, with me - to start throwing questions at him. What'll work better than that is for him to spend a morning working with us, as if he were one of us. We'll get together this afternoon to see what we think."

"The important thing is for you to like him," ventured Nathalie.

"No – the important thing is for all of us to like him. I learnt that from the Umeni. If we decide Ian stays on, we'll be spending even more time with him than we do with our own families, so we'll have to choose with our heads and hearts."

The new customer assistant smiled.

Minutes later, the doors of Captain Flint slid mechanically open. It was the first Monday of December, and more was going to happen than they could possibly imagine.

The happiest company in the world

20.
More interviews

The new employee was due to arrive for his trial run at Captain Flint. Felix went over to John Silver, where in spite of the important change in staff, the flow of clients hadn't slowed.

Elena and Austin, the intellectuals, who were now at the large store, had made way for Gertrude, who'd led the business like an orchestra conductor ever since her colleague had left.

Felix sometimes lent a hand, but often she had to work on her own, managing the stock, tidying the tables and looking after orders for the confused customers,, who rummaged around the tables, bumping into each other.

"How're you doing?" he asked her, slightly concerned.

"Not so bad, surprisingly!" she said with a broad smile. "At first I thought it'd be too much for me, but I've realised the people who come into John Silver don't need too much help. They like whiling away their time here and browsing with the jazz in the background. The atmosphere is already made, you just have to make sure you don't get in their way. Maybe check on them and bring some novelties from time to time ..."

Gertrude showed him a new free corner, where there were thermos flasks of coffee and tea, and mugs so that the customers could serve themselves. A tin with a slit in the top advertised the price of each mug: 1 euro, free for book buyers.

"Can you believe this simple detail has given us a 25% rise in sales?" she said proudly. "We get the same amount of people coming in, but once they've got their mugs, many of them prefer to buy a book and get their tea or coffee for free."

"What a great idea, Gertrude!"

"I'm just a bit worried about the reading club," she said. "The next one's on Thursday, and I've never done anything like that."

"I'll do it for you," Felix volunteered. "Anyway, we're picking a new assistant to cover Jonathan's vacancy, and Jonathan is going to do wonders with our website instead. The new guy is probably starting right now at Captain Flint, but he'll be coming by here to give you a hand before lunchtime. It's vitally important that you feel comfortable with him, and that you can make a good team together."

"A good duo, more like..." said Gertrude. "Alright then, I'll make sure he feels happy here, and let's see how he gets along."

Felix then went into the small storeroom, where phone orders were taken. While he dialled the second candidate from the pile of C.V.'s number, he thought how much Gertrude had changed since she'd come to John Silver.

The happiest company in the world

In the small, familiar bookshop, with all the things she had to attend to, Gertrude had become a fabulous host. Over the years, the monotony of her job at Captain Flint had slowly dampened her spark, and now it had come back to life.

A pleasant female voice answered the phone. Felix told her why he was calling, and she answered his first questions easily.

When he asked about her previous jobs, she hesitated.

"There was a really bad atmosphere, and I ended up resigning," she said.

Felix couldn't help thinking that she could have been part of the bad atmosphere problem.

"They were very happy with me at my last job, but the company had to cut back on its staff and I was unlucky," she concluded.

Felix's biologist's intuition told him there were some people who things always went wrong for. He decided to try the third candidate, a young man with a degree in philosophy, which was a promising start. He'd been involved in cultural projects in several different countries, too.

The first question in the interview came from the candidate.

"Before we go on, can you tell me what the financial conditions are?"

Felix found his demanding attitude a little surprising, but told him the gross yearly salary and working hours before he asked his own first question.

"What are you aiming for professionally?"

"In the mid term, I'd like to travel the world. I'm looking for academic exchange programmes that help educate people in philosophy."

"That's a really interesting idea," answered Felix, "but why would you be interested in a job at a bookshop, then?"

"The foreign exchange programmes I'm looking at could take two or three years to get going. I'm looking for something to do meanwhile so I can save up some money."

"I understand. Thanks for your time and your sincerity."

Felix had no need to carry on asking. A happy company shouldn't consider people who want to work at *something*. It needs someone who will add his or her passion to the team.

KEY 6:
A happy company must have a "why" to identify with.

Happiness in your job and life lies in finding a meaning for what you do. That is what allows you to grow and overcome your difficulties.

Nietzsche said famously, "He who has a why to live can bear almost any how." The "why" is the mission of the company, and we need to feel in tune with it.

In a company or a professional project of our own, we need to know why we've chosen what we did, and how we can stand out in it.

With a team, a common aim – the company's why – will help us improve and make a happy company. As Mark Twain said, "The two most important days in your life are the day you are born and the day you find out why."

LOVE THE WHY OF YOUR COMPANY

21.
The new cabin boy

ELENA
Captain Flint calling John Silver.
The new pirate is sailing towards your seas
for his second boarding.

FELIX
Ahoy there!
How was the sailing this morning?

ELENA
A few incidents
but they were forgiveable.
Cabin boy Ian could become
a good sailor.

FELIX
What kind of incidents?

ELENA
Well, he's a sweet boy,

The happiest company in the world

but a bit blind -
he took off his glasses for the photo.
He crashed into Austin's trolley
and a customer, too,
who nearly fell flat on his face.

         FELIX
         Oh!
        How did he react?

ELENA
The customer or the cabin boy?
Ian apologised profusely
then helped the customer find a few books.

         FELIX
       Did he find his way
      in the thousands of books?

ELENA
Perfectly — he's great at that.
He found everything straight away.
He had a look at the computer
while Nathalie was in the storeroom
and figured out the program straight away.

                              FELIX
                            Wonderful.
                How did he get on with all of you?

ELENA
Very sweet, though he mixed up
all our names.
He called Peter, Austin
and me, Nathalie.
But he's got thousands of book titles
in his head,
just like me.

                              FELIX
                    A clumsy genius, then.

ELENA
Yeah, but he can get better.
He'll learn our names in time.
When he knows the space
he won't bump into anyone anymore.

                              FELIX
            Seems like he made a good impression. ☺

The happiest company in the world

ELENA
Peter says he reminds him of his nephew,
a librarian, also a bit clumsy.
Nathalie was watching him the whole time.
You know what a perfectionist she is.

FELIX
What did you think of him?

ELENA
Charming.
Just as an assistant, of course...

FELIX
Wait — here he is ;-)
We'll all meet tomorrow
for breakfast.

22.
Yes or No

On Tuesday, the five members of staff met an hour before opening to have breakfast and talk about their experiences with the aspiring candidate.

His time at John Silver, which was where he'd be working if he stayed, had shown Gertrude quite a lot.

"I think he'll settle down really fast. He knows what kind of books all the different publishers work with. He's a bit scatterbrained, but once he gets used to things here he'll fit in just fine."

Felix decided to set an order for the meeting before everyone else chipped in with their opinions on Ian's work at Captain Flint.

"I know each of us has something to say, but I suggest we use the binary test so that we can come to some clear conclusions."

Silence fell at the table. Nathalie grimaced and it was obvious not everyone trusted such a simple method of testing a candidate's suitability.

The happiest company in the world

"The Umeni insisted that it's really important to be able to answer all of the questions with a "yes" or "no". Many issues in life are as simple as that, and we ought to be able to get to that kind of synthesis. The first thing I'd ask is, does Ian make you feel comfortable when he's with you at work?"

Elena and Austin nodded.

"I don't know him well enough to say," argued Nathalie.

"I feel comfortable with him," said Gertrude, "and my opinion is worth double the rest – after all, I'm the one who'd be putting up with him and his absent-mindedness all day."

Felix smiled, but reiterated that all of their opinions carried exactly the same weight.

"If Ian joins us," he continued with his next question, "will we be able to provide better quality?"

"Certainly," said Gertrude. "To begin with, I won't have to spend so much time alone. Christmas is just around the corner! And as for Ian himself, he knows a lot and is pleasant, so he'll give customers a better experience."

"I think so too," said Elena.

"It's worth a three-week trial, at least," added Austin. "If we're wrong, we'll be facing the Christmas rush with one less helper."

Nathalie nodded.

"But if we're right, we'll have incorporated an important asset to our company," said Felix. "And now for the third and final question in the binary test. Does today's experience with Ian make you think he fits into our company values?"

"Let's go back and remember them," said Elena. "One: *We love books*. I think that's quite obvious from his photo."

They all laughed and nodded.

"Two: *We like discovering and sharing treasures.*"

"In just a few hours at John Silver, Ian recommended half a dozen books," said Gertrude. "I can guarantee he likes sharing good reads."

"Three," said Elena. "*We make happy moments.*"

Felix then took over.

"It's a bit too soon to know whether or not Ian will make happy moments for us. We'd have to give him a three-week trial period to find that out. How about it?"

They all nodded their assent.

KEY 7:

In order to say yes to what is truly important, companies need to know how to say no.

The YES/NO test is fundamental in all areas of a business, not only in hiring new members for the team.

Bringing in new people is a transcendental decision; but there are other areas where it's sometimes important to say NO.

A happy company needs to know how to say NO to clients, suppliers and opportunities that don't fit in to its values – perhaps because they bring in no profits, perhaps because they don't respect people or the planet we live on.

Learning how to say NO in such cases is a good investment. It helps us focus more on the things that will help us to grow as a company and as people.

LEARN TO SAY NO

23.
Happy reading

Ian's introduction to the workplace freed Felix up to meet Jonathan on Friday. After his new design for the traffic lights program, he'd asked him to make a more creative, more interactive website for both of the stores. A digital platform that would turn from being a flat, soulless page into a place that reflected their company values.

The biologist and the newly-baptised freelance web designer had arranged to meet again at the large park, where they could enjoy the timid rays of the December sun.

Strolling under the bare trees with their fallen leaves rustling underfoot was inspirational for both of them.

"The first problem we need to solve," said Jonathan as they slowly walked along, absorbed in their thoughts, "is that there are two different stores, with different names... and they both have to fit into a single website."

"I've also thought about that," said Felix, pushing his hands into his parka pockets. "We need a name for both of them together. The question to ask when we choose our domain is, what characterises us as booksellers?"

"You want to make your customers happy."

The happiest company in the world

"*We* want," said Felix. "You might be working from home, but you're still with us on board."

Jonathan smiled gratefully and ran his hands through his curly hair like Aladin polishing his lamp.

"I'd stay away from *thehappybookshop.com*. With all respect, it sounds like an oriental bazaar. Anyway, the space isn't the most important thing – it's what you want to happen in it that counts," he said, suddenly inspired.

"We want people to read good books," said Felix.

"Well then, how about *happyreading.com*?"

"Not bad... but it sounds a bit like a website for people who like reading, not a bookshop."

"That's the best thing we could ask for," rejoined Jonathan enthusiastically. "The stores are there, and we can always receive orders online, but what will give our web value is how much traffic there is on it. The more posts, opinions and recommendations we get, the more useful and worthwhile *happyreading.com* will be."

"You're taking the name for granted!" smiled Felix. "We'll have a night out at the bowling rink tomorrow night to celebrate the good news. Why don't you come along and tell the others about the domain?"

"Sure! But let me just tell you why I like that name. The happiest bookshop in the world, which is what we're after, should give readers satisfaction, and things should work by word of mouth. Who could do that better than our readers recommending their favourite books?"

Jonathan came to a stop under a huge plantain whose leaves had all drifted to the ground. He looked up at the sun filtering through its dry branches and said,

"What about *wordofmouth.com*?"

"It's easily remembered, isn't it?" Felix agreed. "But I feel like it takes you away from the idea of a bookshop."

"Maybe... Shall we talk about it tomorrow?" suggested Jonathan.

"Are you any good at bowling?"

"Better at it than customer assistance," Jonathan smiled wanly.

24.
Flight of the geese

A party of nine met for their Saturday celebration. Six members of staff, one of them on trial, Jonathan, Felix, and Simon sat down at one of the tables beside the bowling rink.

The happiest company in the world

Simon seemed surprised at the laughs and companionship he saw.

Happyreading.com won by seven votes as their domain name, and they all ordered hamburgers and chips while they discussed what content to include.

"We should definitely order user recommendations by genre," advised Gertrude. "So readers of niche literature like romance or science fiction won't be bothered by reviews they don't want."

"It might be an idea to set up a competition for the best review," Ian added timidly. "The prize could be a set of books."

"Competitions always work," said Jonathan. "I guess the readers themselves could vote for the best one as they get published."

They carried on chatting animatedly until dinner was over. Jonathan took note of all their ideas so he could send them his first designs in a couple of weeks. They'd set themselves the ambitious task of launching the site on 1st January.

As the bowling began, Simon couldn't resist asking a question that had been bugging him the whole evening.

"You were saying tonight is a celebration. Is there something I should know about?"

"Sales at Captain Flint have risen by more than fifty percent," said Peter proudly.

"That's not hard!" joked Gertrude. "They were virtually non-existent to begin with. John Silver has sold twenty-five percent more, and we had really good customers before."

"Well then, let's celebrate both," said Simon, slightly sceptical.

He hadn't finished the November accounts, but they weren't looking promising.

"At the happiest company in the world," said Felix, "we solve our problems and celebrate our victories together. We're a tribe with a single mission. That's what makes us strong. It reminds me of a study on the flight of geese I did at university."

"Fascinating topic," joked Elena gently as the first bowls were rolling down the wooden floor.

"It's more interesting than you think... Geese can teach us an important lesson with the way they fly. Like other migrating birds, they fly thousands of kilometres each year from their breeding grounds in summer to their winter resting places, and then go back to where they came from." Felix looked hard at Elena, who was studying him through her plastic-rimmed glasses. "Did you know that geese form

The happiest company in the world

flocks of up to a thousand members, and that they fly in a V-shape?"

"No. You mean 'V' for victory?"

"Right," he winked. "Studies show that in that formation, each goose uses the flight of the next. When one flaps its wings, the air moves in such a way that it helps the one behind it. When you get a thousand of them flying like that, the flock travels seventy percent faster and more efficiently than if each bird were to fly alone."

"What happens when one of them flies out of the flock?"

"It notices the air resistance straight away, and realises it's harder alone, so it goes back to its trusted group, makes the most of the strength of the birds in front of it, and helps the ones behind it."

KEY 8:

A trusting environment will create a happy surroundings.

Trusting in our projects, in the philosophy and values of our company and the people who work there is a basic ingredient for a happy company.

Rather than building up a rigid hierarchy, we can show trust by giving each member of a team their autonomy and allowing them to develop their own ideas at work, valuing each person's contributions equally.

The Pygmalion effect states that we will behave according to others' and our own expectations. That is, people will respond to what's expected of them. If we trust our team, our founders, our suppliers and customers, we'll build a truly happy environment and generate passion and enthusiasm.

Trust is not something that can be given half-heartedly. You either trust or you don't. And happy companies choose to trust people who inspire trust in them.

TRUST

25.
The quoting game

On December 10th the group initiated Elena's idea of printing t-shirts with the best quote from the book they were reading.

To stimulate customers' curiosity, they'd decided to print the writer's initials, not his or her full name, beneath the quote. Ian's t-shirt was noticed by the first readers who came in.

"You certainly usually find something,
if you look,
but it is not always quite the something you were after"
J.R.R.T.

"Is that from *The Hobbit*?" asked a spotty teenager with rings under her eyes.

"Bingo! You got it! You must know Tolkien by heart! Have you also got the anthology of the letters and poems he wrote? It might not be what you were looking for, but you've just chanced upon it!"

Gertrude smiled as she looked at him out of the corner of her eye. The new guy was good at connecting any questions with a book which would end up being purchased.

She'd decided to make an unashamed statement with a quote she'd treasured since she was a young girl and had read *Little Women*.

Be worthy, love, and love will come.
L.M.A.

Only two of the assistants at John Silver's big sister store had chosen their quote. Peter had chosen a slightly old-fashioned romantic sentence that he identified with from *The Shadow of the Wind*, by Carlos Ruíz Zafón.

When I die, everything that's mine will be yours
except for my dreams.
C.R.Z.

Elena, the instigator, had chosen a sentence from *Tokyo Blues,* her favourite novel by the most successful Japanese writer in the West.

I would touch a familiar book and draw its fragrance deep
inside me.
This was enough to make me happy.

The happiest company in the world

H.M.

Over the next few days, Nathalie and Austin also got their t-shirts made, and the game between them and the readers became unexpectedly popular.

Customers would stop in front of an assistant and try to guess the author of the quote by the initials under it. The most expert readers even tried to guess which book it was from, and they would proudly tell the assistant.

The conversation would often end with the book being sold, and so the storeroom had to be kept stocked with any of the quoted titles.

A local radio mentioned the game and brought in even more curious customers.

The staff at the two bookshops were no longer mere sellers. The t-shirts showed a piece of their souls, and they'd become promises of happiness in the shape of books.

26.
The fourth value

One week later, Austin asked the whole team to meet up again for lunch. Since Captain Flint had taken in its new members the store seemed to be buzzing with ideas.

"Call me sentimental, but there's only one week left to go before Christmas, and I was thinking that maybe our three values aren't quite enough."

Felix liked the fact that Austin, who'd always been quite reserved, was daring to express his opinions so clearly.

"What values do you think are missing, Austin?"

"Well, the three first ones we set are about our customer's happiness and our own. And that's all very well, but there are people out there whose circumstances make going into bookshops impossible for them. I'd like to do something for those people."

"That sounds amazing," said Elena.

Everyone else nodded, while Felix's scientific mind insisted on clarifying Austin's aim.

"What kind of people would like to read but can't get their hands on any books? Do you mean some kind of cooperation with the third world?"

The happiest company in the world

"There's no need to look that far," said Austin, stroking his beard. "There are people right here in the city who can never go into a store to buy a book they'd love, or do a lot of other things, either. There's an initiative in some bars called "Owe Me A Coffee" which gets people to buy a hot coffee for homeless people who are out in the cold. And," he murmured, "there are two groups that come to mind when I think of books. One of them is long-term hospital patients, especially elderly people who're lonely and may not get a lot of visitors. There are libraries in the big hospitals, but I don't think they have all that many recent publications. The patients can't keep in touch with what's going on and so they start to feel more and more out of touch with the world."

An admiring silence followed his explanation. They were all moved by the idea, though it was hard to see right then how they could put it into practice. Jonathan was the first to come up with a suggestion. He'd joined them at lunch so he could show them some of his new web designs.

"I think it'd be a waste of time to pack boxes of books that nobody would want to read. All we'd do is gather stuff like old cooking books that haven't been used for the last twenty years, or Part 2 of some series with Part 1 missing."

"Good thinking," interjected Austin. "Why shouldn't people in hospitals or prisons be able to choose what they want to read just like our customers? Our role would be to help them out with that as much as we could."

"How do you think we could manage that?" asked Felix enthusiastically.

That day, more than any other since he'd come back to "civilization", Felix felt proud of his tribe. He thought about how lucky he was to be in a group that had put forward an initiative like this one in their free time.

"I'll start with what I can do," offered Jonathan. "I think one very obvious possibility would be to make a section at *happyreading.com* where people could say exactly what books they'd like to have and give others a chance to buy them for them."

"But that shouldn't just be on the web," added Gertrude. "Let's imagine we had five requests, say – we could exhibit the books at the store and add a note from everyone who's asked for them. If we put them near the till, I bet more than one customer would be prepared to chip in."

"That seems like a great idea to me," said Felix, overjoyed. "Now all that's left is to figure out how we could get the books to those who need them; but that's just a matter of logistics. Now, let's write down what we've just thought up."

The happiest company in the world

Together, just like that, they defined the fourth value of the happiest company in the world.

We like making our work meaningful.

27.
The Loewenstein experiment

Over the next few days, Felix felt slightly overwhelmed. So much was happening at the same time. After thirty years of lethargy, the stores had suddenly turned into a breeding ground for ideas, and he was scared things might get out of hand in the Christmas frenzy.

In the kitchen of the small flat he'd just rented, he wrote down all the different initiatives underway:

1. Renovating Captain Flint (large portraits of writers, new space for reading clubs as of December).
2. Stating company values (4).
3. Relocating staff to give them enjoyable new experiences (successful so far).
4. Bringing a new member into the team (Ian, in the final week of his trial period).
5. Initiative to get new publications to people who can't buy books.

The happiest company in the world

Felix sipped his mint tea and thought that if Simon had been there, he'd have criticised his aims and achievements for not including improving company finances.

But the biologist had learnt from the Umeni that when you seek the common good, abundance is a natural consequence. You couldn't mess with that order.

So, instead of saying "Let's see what we can do to earn money," he preferred to say, "Let's see what we can do to generate value," which would bring the clients in and end up benefiting them financially.

As he thought about this, Felix read a page from a book Austin had recommended him, *A Storytale Life,* whose writer, Elena Mateos, was talking about an experiment similar to the one they'd started up at the busiest moment in the year.

Between 2005 and 2010, American economist George F. Loewenstein focused his research on the emotional effects produced by two opposing attitudes: greed and generosity. To begin with, he chose sixty people of different ages, genders, races and professions. Then he divided the members of his sociological experiment into two groups of thirty. Each of them were given $6,000. Members of the first group were asked to spend their money in two months on gifts to themselves. Meanwhile, the second group were asked to spend it on gifts for other people.

Two months later, two opposing sets of results were achieved. The first group's satisfaction hadn't lasted for long. The conclusion was that after their initial euphoria in buying, using and possessing certain consumer goods, participants very soon returned to their normal way of feeling. As the days went by, some of them even started feeling sad, empty and disheartened as they could no longer maintain the excitement of their purchase.

The other group, though, felt much more satisfied and fulfilled than the first. Having to think about how they could use their money to benefit others made them feel good inside. Most of them used the $6,000 to pay for others to travel, on university fees, on donations to non-profit organisations; they gave it out to the homeless or helped family members out with their debts. After presenting their gifts, their joy and the gratitude of others gave them an intense feeling of fulfilment which lasted for hours, even days, according to Loewenstein.

The conclusion was obvious, thought Felix. To make the company the happiest in the world, its spirit had to extend

> The happiest company in the world

beyond the confines of the bookshops and be given a deeper meaning.

KEY 9:
The ultimate aim of a company is to improve the society it works in.

Our self-esteem is closely linked to how useful we feel to the world around us. All of us like to see how the things we do improve others' lives. The happiest company in the world should aim to generate value for everyone from its customers to its staff.
Steven Covey's "win-win", where everyone benefits, is the best formula for success.
Working for the common good is a powerful motivation for any business project.
Musician Pau Casals once said in one of his most famous speeches, "You must work – we all must work – to make the world a better place for our children."

IMPROVE SOCIETY

28.
Christmas Eve

It was Christmas Eve. Felix suddenly realised something that hadn't occurred to him before. He'd been so busy getting the bookshops back on their feet – sales had risen exponentially – that he'd forgotten he was going to be alone on the most important family occasion of the year.

He'd seen so little of his dad, and then his dad had died; and after that, his only living relatives were his aunts and uncles and the cousins who lived in other cities. Apart from seeing his colleagues at work, it looked like he'd be spending Christmas alone.

Felix heated up a quarter roast chicken in the microwave, and thought back nostalgically to his life among the Umeni. Being alone was unthinkable for the tribe, who did absolutely everything together. They surely would have felt sorry for him had they known he'd be spending such a special night all alone except for his TV and stereo.

He zapped around for a bit and then turned off the TV and put on an album by Ella Fitzgerald. Then he sat down to watch the stars in the clear night sky from his sofa.

The happiest company in the world

He'd rented a thirty square metre loft, whose smallness was compensated by the view of the heavens stretching out above him.

Ella was singing her sensual *Dream a Little Dream of Me* when his phone notified him that a message had come in.

He waited, his eyes dreamily half-closed, for the song to end before checking to see who it was.

ELENA
I don't want to be cliché, but...
Happy Christmas!
Have a lovely time with your family.

FELIX
Happy Christmas to you too!
I don't know if it's lovely or not
but I'm celebrating it on my own.

ELENA
Oh!
☹

FÉLIX
Well, not quite on my own -
a beautiful woman from Virginia is here with me:

Ella Fitzgerald.

ELENA
Sounds good.☺
If it's any consolation,
I'm also celebrating Xmas Eve
almost on my own.

FELIX
Almost?
What do you mean?

ELENA
I'm at my mum's,
we're alone here,
but she doesn't know I'm with her.
Well, from time to time she does -
when I hold her hand,
she smiles sometimes
and her eyes shine so I know
she remembers something.

The happiest company in the world

Felix's eyes welled with tears. He'd also held his mum's hand through her slow agony before he went off to the Amazon.

Also, he was beginning to realise that he liked Elena more than he'd been willing to admit.

FELIX

She knows who you are the whole time, Elena.
Even with advanced Alzeimer's, if that's what she has.
In her own way, your mum knows
you're with her
and that makes her happy.

FELIX
Still there?

ELENA
Yeah, sorry.
I was feeling a bit emotional.
By the way, I have an idea.

FELIX
Is it a really good one?
I've gotten used to hearing really good ones!

ELENA
How about if you came over
and spent Xmas Eve with us?

The happiest company in the world

29.
Holding hands

The flat Elena and her mother shared was at the top of the city. Felix nearly froze while he waited half an hour for a taxi to pull up, but finally managed to get to their peculiar party.

Mother and daughter were sitting on the sofa. There was a difference of about forty years between them, but they were watching a German channel together, which was going around the world to see how Christmas was celebrated in different parts of the world, from Siberia to Tahiti, to a remote village in the Andes.

The old woman seemed to be hypnotized by the flow of idyllic images with their bright figures and children singing. But her face was as rigid as a stone figure.

Elena, by her side, had a copy of *The Heart is a Lonely Hunter* next to her with her glasses sitting on top of it.

She gave Felix a kiss on the cheek, and told her mum they had a guest. The old woman reacted with a slight head movement, and Elena moved up to make room for Felix.

"It's been a long time since I had a family session in front of the TV," joked Felix. "The closest thing I've done since my mum died was watching the fire with the Amazon tribe I lived with."

"That's pretty much what we do here. My mum doesn't understand anything that happens on the TV, and nor do I, mostly. It's kind of like a digital fire to light us up and help us feel less lonely tonight."

A strange emotion ran through Felix's chest as he heard her. Wanting to hide his nervousness, he went into the kitchen to open a bottle of champagne he'd brought with him. He filled the three empty glasses standing on the table in front of the sofa.

On a windowsill was a tiny Christmas tree whose lights blinked rhythmically.

"I'm sorry to have brought you all the way here," said Elena. "I guess it's not such a joyful celebration in this flat."

"I'm really happy to be here, I promise you. It's so much better than sitting at home alone. I'd probably be asleep by now."

Elena smiled. "Well, what would be so bad about that? Can I ask you a question, Felix? Are you happy?"

"I really don't know how to answer that," he replied, flustered. "It depends on the day, doesn't it."

"I mean, are you happy with your new life?" she insisted. "It sounds like you really loved your life in Brazil,

The happiest company in the world

your research, your little lab... Don't you ever regret having picked up from where your father left off?"

"Not at all," he said, taking a sip of his champagne. "There's nowhere better I could be than here, on this adventure we're all on together. And there's nowhere I'd want to be this Christmas more than right here, with you."

"Really?" she asked in surprise. "What makes that so special?"

Felix took a deep breath. "Well, now that we're not at work, but here at your home, I can say, what's special about this Christmas for me is to be sitting here next to you. That's more than enough for me."

Elena took his hand in answer and held it warmly in hers.

The old woman suddenly started stuttering agitatedly, asking for the attention she hadn't been given in a while.

Her daughter listened happily as the words came out. The TV was showing a celebration in Bahia, and she heard, "I can see people... a lot of people."

Elena took her mother's small, shrunken hand, while her other hand stayed clasped around Felix's. A tear slid slowly down her trembling cheek.

Felix felt like the sofa was a raft floating in the ocean of the world, with the three of them on it doing a motionless dance as old as time itself.

30.
Happiness is a puzzle

Back in his flat in the early hours of the morning, Felix couldn't get to sleep. A strong feeling was welling inside him and he could do nothing to stop it. And the worst thing was, he felt afraid.

Sooner or later, he'd reveal his love to Elena, and her answer would be like life or death to him. He hadn't fallen in love since his early years at University, when the relationship had wilted after a promising start. "We're too different," she'd told him, and broken up with him right then.

Would Elena feel the same way? She clearly liked him, but perhaps she'd see him as an oddity who fit in better to his jungle hamlet than to the city.

A message came in to his phone, and his nerves tingled in anticipation. But it wasn't her.

The happiest company in the world

Happy Christmas, Felix.
Thanks so much for helping me find my real passion.
I feel more and more like this is the path I must follow.
You know something? I'd always been scared to go freelance,
in case I couldn't work things out and live off it.
But now I've learnt that almost everything that happens depends on me.
And that there are amazing people who help us along, of course.
Like you and the others, Felix.
Thanks for helping me do what I always wanted, but didn't know I did.
A big hug to you,

Jonathan.

Felix returned the message, thanking Jonathan for his kindness and wishing him a happy Christmas, and then tucked himself under two blankets and picked up his book of short stories from the table. Before he went to sleep, he read a contemporary fable by an unknown author.

The story was about a scientist who, like Felix, was worried about the world's problems. Wanting to find solutions to them, he spent entire days shut up in his lab, just like him, looking for answers.

One day his seven-year-old son came into his lab and asked him if he could help out.

The scientist was annoyed at being interrupted, and told the boy to go and play outside. But the boy wouldn't listen, and so he thought up a way to entertain him and let him get on with his research.

The boy's father took a pair of scissors and cut a map in a magazine into small pieces, which he gave to his son.

"I know you like puzzles, so why don't you put together this picture of the world? It's all in pieces, but let's see if you can do it on your own."

The scientist had cut up the map really small, and thought it would take his son hours to put it together again. But in just a short while, the boy came back with it, and set it down enthusiastically in front of him.

"Look, dad, I've done it!"

"You can't have..."

He was sure his son couldn't have put together a map he'd never seen before, but he looked up and saw the puzzle, which was taped together.

To his surprise his son had managed to do it perfectly. The father put aside what he was doing.

The happiest company in the world

"How did you manage to do that so fast?" he asked the boy, "when you've never even seen a picture of the world?"

"I haven't, and I didn't know what it looked like. But on the other side of the paper there was a picture of a man. So I just turned the pieces around and started sticking the man together, because I knew what he looked like. And when I turned it all over again, I saw I'd fixed the world, too. Look how fantastic it is!"

Felix turned out the light with the pleasant feeling that the night wasn't so cold, after all. Nobody can feel alone when they can help someone else, he thought to himself as his eyes closed.

31.
The nomination

The last Saturday of the month came with two pieces of news, one good, one bad. The good one news was that John Silver and Captain Flint had been nominated as "best bookshops" in the country by a specialised magazine.

"The final results will be out on the 11th January," Felix told Gertrude on a visit to the little sister of the two stores, "so we can find out then whether we still have reason to celebrate."

"My news isn't so great," announced Jonathan, who was updating the small bookshop's search system. "Look at the green light graph for December."

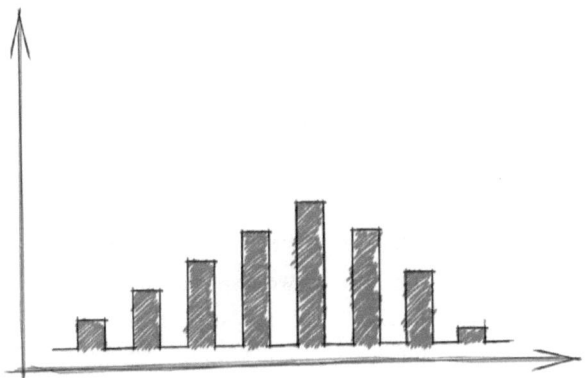

The happiest company in the world

"Why do you think people aren't feeling so satisfied anymore?" Felix asked Ian, who was making a promising start to his final three-month test run at the store.

"My opinion as a new arrival is that they're exhausted by the new initiatives, plus the normal Christmas rush."

"Do you feel tired? Tell me sincerely, please."

"No, but I've only been here for three weeks or so," he shrugged. "Everyone else has been working here the whole year, and I think it's quite normal for them to be fading a bit right now."

"We can't let up until King's Day on the 6th January," said Gertrude. "There's still time to sell a lot of books. We can rest after the 7th, if there aren't too many returns, that is..."

"But there are still nearly ten days to go for that," murmured Felix. "I reckon we need a breath of fresh air, don't you? We'll run out of oxygen if we don't get one. Are we supposed to be opening tomorrow?"

"Yes, in the afternoon," said Ian. "We're running up to King's Day, remember. And we decided we'd spend Sunday morning organizing our stocks a bit."

"Well, I think the stock can wait until Monday. We'll take a trip out at lunchtime so we can all relax for a while. What do you think?"

Ian and Gertrude gave the thumbs up. Jonathan said he'd go with them. Then they called the others at Captain Flint to let them know.

All of them agreed that the world wasn't going to come to an end if the store didn't open on Sunday morning.

KEY 10:

The values of a happy company should agree with its staff's.

As well as working together to achieve as much creativity, excellence and effectiveness as possible, the values that a company

The happiest company in the world transmits should coincide with it's staff's so that the people who work in it can feel happy.

A pacifist will never feel at home working for an arms manufacturer or at a bank which invests in it. Anyone sensitive to children's rights can never work authentically at a company which has factories with child labour in third world countries.

Shared ethics and common values are basic for happiness in everything we do with other people.

Roy E. Disney, the last member of the family to be involved in his father and uncle's company, said, "When your values are clear to you, making decisions becomes easier."

ALIGN YOUR VALUES WHIT THOSE OF YOUR COMPANY

32.
Steaming with ideas

All of the team except for Simon, who didn't like the December cold, departed in two cars at eight the following morning for a spa in the mountains.

It was forty kilometres away from the city, and if they were lucky they'd manage to spend a couple of hours in the thermal waters before having lunch and going back; but all of them felt like it would help them refresh.

"With this cold, refreshing is an understatement!" complained Austin as he got out of the car. "It must be below zero here."

They picked up their towels and bathrobes from the counter, and then came out of their different changing rooms and slipped into a natural pool fed by underground springs.

"This is heaven..." groaned Peter as he felt the thirty-six degree water envelop him. "I really needed something like this after all those weeks behind the till. Man does not live on books alone..."

Meanwhile, the others paddled around in the sulphurous water, lay belly-up or played at pushing each other under.

The happiest company in the world

The games and laughter faded into a state so pleasant they nearly fell asleep. Ian made the most of the relaxed atmosphere and asked, "What do you expect from me over the next three months?"

"Make us fall in love with you," Felix joked.

"He's already done that," said Gertrude. "What I'd like is for you to learn how to manage the six reading clubs programmed for the first term of the year."

Ian sunk down into the water in response, coming up seconds later between Nathalie and Elena, who screamed in fake surprise.

After a brief chat, Elena swam slowly and lazily over to Felix's side. He smiled happily.

"What a great idea it was to come here," she said. "It'll get us up and running again until the end of the Christmas period."

"It wasn't me who chose this place. Peter suggested it. He comes here once a year with his wife to celebrate their wedding anniversary. Apparently they did their wedding party here, too."

"It's great they still come here, don't you think?" said Elena. "It must be so nice to see how the years go by and turn to decades with the person you love by your side."

"I think that's something to aspire to."

"Yeah, but it's so hard..."

They floated together with their heads above water in their swimming caps and looked straight at each other, smiling timidly.

"Saving the stores also looked like it was going to be really hard, but Simon told me yesterday we'd be closing the year with much better results than expected," said Felix. "Nothing is easy or difficult in itself. It's us who make it one or the other."

"What have you decided to do?" she asked.

"About what?"

"About love, of course?"

Just then, at the worst possible moment, Jonathan came swimming up with a new idea.

"I know how we can make *happyreading.com* the most influential book blog in the country. We'll post reviews and video-reviews on YouTube, so we can add our own followers to the web," he said excitedly. "And I'll make a section called, 'I was there', just for people who come to the reading clubs. And finally, a 'Greatest Hits' section for books of all times that can change your life. That's almost up already."

"There are only four days left before the end of the year," murmured Felix, put out by the interruption.

The happiest company in the world

"I know, but unless some kind of act of God hits my studio, the web will be up."

33.
Life-changing books

Happyreading.com had its first test run on the web the day before the new year began. There were no reviews or comments on it yet, but all the staff at their computers were pleasantly surprised by Jonathan's section titled, "Greatest hits of all times".

The editor of the blog had resolved to read the following ten books in the new year:

1. MAN'S SEARCH FOR MEANING
Viktor Frankl
An unforgettable reminder of our power to choose, even in the worst of circumstances.

2. THE LITTLE PRINCE
Antoine de Saint-Exupéry
You might have read it as a child, but it doesn't matter. Mature adults will find this essential work to be a lucid, revealing analysis of love and the human condition.

3. TAO TE CHING
Lao-Tse

The happiest company in the world

A founding work of Tao philosophy, whose infinitely interpreted poems hold the highest wisdom of the East.

4. DON QUIXOTE
Miguel de Cervantes
Richly written and full of comical predicaments. A great lesson in the strength of idealism.

5. HOW TO MAKE FRIENDS AND INFLUENCE PEOPLE
Dale Carnegie
A handbook for excelling at human relationships. First published in 1936, and still as useful as ever!

6. SIDDHARTHA
Hermann Hesse
The best introduction to Buddhism and other Eastern traditions, told with the simplicity of a young adult novel.

7. THE SEVEN HABITS OF HIGHLY EFFECTIVE PEOPLE
Stephen Covey
A modern classic for understanding how to manage your business and life (We had to make this No. 7).

8. COUNT YOUR BLESSINGS
John Demartini

A self-improvement book for understanding the power of gratitude and its capacity to transform every aspect of your life.

9. THE DIARY OF ANNE FRANK
Anne Frank

The most famous, most moving diary ever written. Proof of how purity and goodness can withstand even the worst moments.

10. GOOD LUCK
Álex Rovira & Fernando Trías de Bes

A tale which tells how to create favourable circumstances, and simply and graphically illustrates the attitudes that will make a difference in any life project.

11. CRUCIAL CONVERSATIONS: TOOLS FOR TALKING WHEN STAKES ARE HIGH
K. Patterson, J. Grenny, R. McMillan, A. Switzler

An effective guide to assertive communication in your personal and professional life.

The happiest company in the world

A fundamental reference for any couple or business seeking happiness.

34.
Twelve

It was New Years Eve, and Felix was even more nervous than on the morning the hydroplane landed in the jungle where he'd be staying for the next two years.

A distant relative had come to take care of Elena's mum, and she'd proposed they spend the last night of the old year (and the first night of the new one) together.

As Felix walked along the well-lit boulevard with his hands in his pockets, he thought to himself that what happened tonight would determine which way his future went. He was going to take an essential step, and if Elena refused him he didn't know how he'd get over it.

If she did, he thought, he would leave the bookshops in the hands of the team, who no longer needed him, and would go back to his lab in the Amazon.

There was still half an hour to go before the New Year chimed in, and Elena was waiting for him outside a café where people were gathering strength with hot chocolate and biscuits.

She was wearing a red coat and beret to bring in the year, and greeted Felix with a hug that made his heart leap.

The happiest company in the world

He was wondering exactly when in the night he'd be able to show her what he felt for her.

Her small hand in its woollen glove searched for his as they walked towards the main square. Under the city clock, a multitude of people were bracing themselves against the cold to say goodbye to the year and usher in the new one.

"Have you taken a look back yet?" she asked him as they walked. "At this year, I mean."

"Actually, I wouldn't know where to begin, so much has gone on... I had to leave my pharmaceutical project when my dad died, and take over a dying business I knew nothing about."

"I think you've passed with flying colours."

"Really?"

"Everyone at the stores thinks so too," she said energetically.

"Well, I feel like you did it all yourselves," said Felix sincerely. "My only merit was to notice what talents each of you had and get you to do what you know best."

"You brought back our passion, and that changed everything. But... do you really want to end the year talking about work?"

"No, I don't!"

"So then, tell me what your New Year's resolutions are," she pleaded. "And make sure they have nothing to do with work, will you?"

"I'm going to disappoint you, I'm sure..."

"I bet you won't."

"I bet I will – I'm pretty unoriginal," he admitted. "I've made up my mind to eat healthier and do my own cooking. To do sport three times a week. And spend Sundays in the countryside to detox... Things like that. What about you?"

"There's only one thing I want for the New Year, but I'll tell you after the chimes... They're coming just now!"

The enthusiastic crowd watched as the city clock ticked closer and closer to the hour. Less than a minute was left for the ritual to begin and the old year to pass away. Grapes were eaten to the count of the twelve chimes and champagne drunk.

"Have you brought any grapes?" she said.

"Did I have to?" he asked, flustered.

"I thought you were getting them."

"Sorry, I didn't know..."

Seconds were left and nervous shrieks rang out from the crowd as they uncorked their champagne and brought out their bags of grapes.

The happiest company in the world

"Bad luck all year for us," she complained. "Unless, that is, we substitute something else for the grapes."

"What?" asked Felix, confused.

The first chime of the New Year rang out, and Elena leant over and kissed Felix on the lips. And then he knew what she meant.

35.
The happiest bookshop in the world

January 11th was a Monday, but the six members of staff at the two stores were having a celebratory lunch with Felix, Jonathan and Simon, who was sitting proudly at the head of the table.

They'd ordered a catering service to provide the meal at Captain Flint. This was no ordinary party.

Surrounded by thousands of books, with the jazz music from John Silver playing in the background, Felix was the first to speak.

He started with a riddle: "I know there are a lot of things to celebrate today; but I'd like each of you to say why you think we're here."

All of them were moved and nobody said anything for a moment. Nathalie broke the ice.

"We're celebrating because after a lot of beating around the bush, you finally managed to make things happen with Elena."

The rest of the staff broke into applause, and Elena's cheeks turned bright red. In spite of her embarrassment, she took Felix's hand.

The happiest company in the world

Ian was the next to speak, and he carried on in the same jocular tone.

"We're celebrating because even though my three-month trial period isn't over yet, you've fallen in love with me and want me to stay here as long as our passion and enthusiasm lasts."

More applause followed.

"It's my turn now," said Simon. "I do the numbers, and they're never wrong. I'd like you all to know that sales in December were 50 percent higher than in December the year before." The accountant paused and then went on, "And the January slump hasn't begun all that badly. We're still selling, and don't depend as much on our loan. Our figures are getting stronger."

"That's the way we want it - strong and squeaky clean," said Peter, who was feeling the effects of the wine.

When the laughter had died down, Felix stood up again.

"I feel especially proud today," he said, "to be here with you all. I've felt proud since the first day I came into the stores, but now, I'm even more so. We've just heard something quite important."

There was silence around the table as Felix pulled out a piece of paper from his pocket and unfolded it.

He read aloud, "The *most important index of cultural businesses* has a list of "Best Bookshops" for the coming year, and they've published us in the "Small and Medium Companies" category, and we're number one! Hundreds of customers have chosen us as the store which provides readers with the best experience. Isn't that great?"

Loud cheers came from all round, and then everyone at the table started hugging and kissing each other.

Under cover of the party atmosphere and feeling of "mission accomplished but not yet over," Simon walked over to Felix and handed him a thick cream-coloured envelope. He gestured enigmatically for Felix to put it away for later, and then went back to his chair.

Felix wondered what the envelope could hold, but gave Simon a hug, saying, "Now we really can say we're the happiest company in the world."

The happiest company in the world

Epilogue:
digging up the treasure

When Felix opened the envelope, he couldn't believe his eyes. It held the greatest treasure he could imagine: an 1883 copy of *Treasure Island*!

Amazed, he slowly turned its yellow pages. Just before the first chapter, he encountered a folded piece of paper written in his father's hand.

Felix felt tears well up behind his eyes as he read the letter, which had been written while he was thousands of kilometres away.

To my son Felix:

I'm leaving this letter with Simon, and have asked him to give it to you when he feels the time is right. I know I've left you a lot of work to do.
After my final journey begins, I'll be sailing towards you in the first edition ever published of Stevenson's novel.

Now that I feel my days are coming to an end, I want to leave you these lines so that you can read them when the tide goes down again. I wanted to explain some things to you that I never did.

You might sometimes have wondered why such an unadventurous man as myself would have wanted to open two different bookshops and name them after characters from Treasure Island.

Let me try to answer.

I chose this business, which as I leave it is about to sink, because books are the only thing that can give you back your life. I say "give back" and not "save", because nothing and nobody except yourself can ever save you. Each of us captains our own ship. What the pages of a book can do is to give you back your hope, which is the wind of life, and your inspiration when storms buffet you.

I chose to sell inspiration, and used Stevenson's novel to baptise the two stores. I've always considered bookshops to be treasure islands. Readers land there in the hope of finding what they need to motivate them and bring them prosperity.

Because of my terrible shyness and gloomy personality, I was never able to transmit these values to my crew, just as I never gave you inspiration when you most needed it.

The happiest company in the world

Luckily, I know you're better than me at that, and at just about everything else.
Please don't ever doubt that I loved you, even if I've never managed to express it until now, when it's too late.
Now that you're at the helm, I know you'll be able to give your crew a helping hand as you sail together to the isle of happiness.

Happy sailing, and don't ever stop following your dreams!

Felix sighed as he put the letter away in his chest of literature. He let the tears course down his cheeks as he thought about his dad's unexpected farewell. A lesson full of beauty and inspiration from a man he wished he could have known better.

Following his most precious dreams with his fellows on board, thought Felix. That would be his motto from now on.

There's no greater treasure than the one you can share with the whole world; but the search begins inside you.

KEY 11:
The happiest company in the world is you.

Many people run their lives as if they were something outside them. They let their happiness depend on whether they meet the right person to love, whether they find the job they dream of, or whether the economy gets better, without realising that every human being is in command of his or her own life.

Thoreau said that "There is no value in life except what you choose to place upon it and no happiness in any place except what you bring to it yourself."

When we sit at the helm of our own life like the captain of a ship, setting our own direction and choosing our colleagues wisely, we take on responsibility for everything that happens to us.

Every person is a company with assets, a mission, profits and losses; but to really know success, the conquest of our own and others' happiness should come before anything else.

THE HAPPY COMPANY IS IN YOU

The happiest company in the world

If you want to build a ship,
don't drum up the men to gather wood,
divide the work, and give orders.
Instead, teach them to yearn
for the vast and endless sea

ANTOINE DE SAINT-EXUPERÝ

Acknowledgements

One of the sayings that has accompanied me throughout the years is Ciceron's quote "Gratitude is not only the greatest of virtues, but the mother of all others."

I consider that every person we come across and every moment we live give us something be thankful for, and I would like to extend my gratitude to all the people who I have met and who have somehow helped me build and create the book "The Happiest Company in the World."

Particularly, I would like to start by thanking my family for their time, support and love, Paloma, Marco and Alnara. To my parents, Ginesa and Pedro, and to Marta and Tamotsu for trusting me to start the project of Cyberclick together.

To all the people who I have worked with at Cyberclick, particularly Sergi, Sol, Ana, Sergio, Estela, Berta, Toni, Nerea, Héctor, Judit, Kelly, Laia, and Anna. To the entrepreneurs of the group, Alberto and Sonia, Xavi, Jordi, and Pau, and the rest of the Cyberclick Group members, integrated by Albert, Alejandra, Ana Mendez, Andratx,

The happiest company in the world

Aniol, Anna Campins, Berta Hernández, Dimitri, Elena, Eva, Federica, Ignasi, Jessica, Jonathan, Jordi Cuenca, Judith, Laura, Marc Cámara, Marc Gilabert, María José, Marina, Marta Dardichon, Marta Torné, Marta Vidal, Mireia, Oriol, Rubén, Sara, Stephanie, Xavi Burguillos, Xavi Pla, and Zorion.

To the friends with whom I have shared experiences and learned so much: Arnaud, Carme, Cristopher, Connor, Jaume, Josep, Raúl, Susana, and Xavi. To Verne Harnish for sharing all his *knowhow* and helping me discover what the best companies in the world do. To a lot of my entrepreneur friends, Jordi Albalate, Juan Carlos Ángeles, Luis Ignacio Cortés, Antonio González-Barros, Lluís Guerra, Joan Mora, Sebastian Ross, Frank Trittel, André Vanyi-Robin, David Boronat, Johan Allund, André Ribeiro, Francesc Ribes and Erik Brieva.

To the partners and friends with whom I have shared the passion of starting a business and supporting entrepreneurs to help them grow their projects: Vicente Arias, Albert Armengol, Iñaki Arrola, Sergio Balcells, Antonio Bernal, Carlos Blanco, Jorge Blasco, Francois Derbaix, Iñaki Ecenarro, Jesús Encinar, Marta Esteve, Lluís Faus, Marek

Fodor, Óscar Fuente, Daniel Giménez, Jaume Gomà, Dídac Lee, Juan Margenat, Sacha Michaud, Jesús Monleón, Mauricio Prieto, Francesc Riverola, Pablo Szefner, and Josep María Tribó.

To the startup founders with whom I have been able to collaborate with and debate about happiness and business: Ángel Corcuera, Joaquim Esteve, Nacho González-Barros, Bart Huisken, Luciano Langenauer, Lucía Layunta, Santos García, Gloria Molins, Víctor Pellerin, David Pérez, Oscar Pierre, Xavier Pladellorens, Karen Prats, Liher del Río.

I also want to thank the friends with whom I have shared a lot of great moments, and who have taught me what great people do: Anna Arreciado, Anna Bolaño, Eva Durán, Silvia Calafell, Albert y Silvia, Pitus, Paco and Azu, Xisco and María, Lluís Llurba and Estefanía. To Francesc Miralles for inspiring me and helping me, and to Carlos Nogales and Laura Romero for sharing with me what happy families do.

To Carmen Mur, Nuria Blasi, and Miquel Cabré for being great mentors and to Óscar Arias, José Ramos-Horta, Gbowee Leymah, Ferran Adrià, Jorge Garbajosa, and Luis

Huete for having the generosity of sharing their time and recommending "The Happiest Company in the World."

To José Tovoli, Nicolás Ramilo and to all the Great Place to Work team. To Sonia de Mier, Álvaro Martínez, Lorena Martínez, and Gema Risco for sharing their opinion of the book and for the enthusiasm they put into making businesses happier everyday.

I still remember when I sent my first email. I didn't know how to finish it and, because I didn't want it to sound too formal, I wrote <<Thank you>>. Since then, I finish all my emails saying thank you, so I want to finish this book with the exact same message.

Reviews

I have enjoyed and learned so much reading this book. It is a very accurate version of how the acquired qualities of a scientist: observation, strictness, creativity, results, and analysis of the information and teamwork, are essential to accomplish an efficient business management.

Núria Basi - President of Armand Basi

If we were capable of proposing a more noble and intelligent way of working, I am sure that we would be able to touch our coworkers and connect with them. This is the challenge that David Tomás has made his at Cyberclick and who has had the generosity to put in black and white in this book. We are all getting a call to be part of the solution to the problems of our times. Thank you David, for being an active agent of the better society we are all seeking.

Luis Huete - IESE Business School Professor

An important book for everyone who believes that people make the results. And even more fundamental for those who don't believe it yet. Inspiring and simple, it explains how actions should be for leaders who aspire to create something better.

José Tovoli - Partner and Board Member of Great Place to Work

David Tomás explains in this book, in a very simple way, the philosophy he applies at Cyberclick, which has led him

The happiest company in the world

to obtain the price for the "Best Company To Work For In Spain. This philosophy looks out for commitment and people who share the company's values and the projects David develops. This book proves that a healthy work environment is not against productivity and business success, and that in fact, it works the opposite way. A very applicable philosophy, in my opinion, to high performance athletics.

Jorge Garbajosa - Spanish ex basketball player

The first time I read the title I thought the book could be kind of idealist and not very practical. However, David's story captured my attention and taught me simple steps leaders can follow to achieve a balance between happiness and productivity at work. A fun story that will shape your leadership decisions in the future years.

Connor Neill - Leadership professor, IESE Business School

I wish there were more people like Felix in the world, the protagonist of the story. Companies would function better if they had leaders like him. To my understanding, the ideas the book proposes are deep, nevertheless, very easy to apply.

Plus, they can be very useful for the day to day of any organization.

Carmen Mur - President of "Fundació Somni dels Nens"

What I have learned in over 30 years of experience educating entrepreneurs, is that companies that create happiness and satisfaction, are the ones that grow faster and have a greater impact. This book describes the key ingredients to create a gratifying work environment for every member of the team.

Verne Harnish - General Director of Gazelles Inc and Founder of Entrepreneurs Organization

The characters in this book are fictional, but the ideas are real. They come from a continuous effort from David to build happy companies and successful - in this particular order - and this way, make the world a better place. Even if after reading this story you only take away one of the proverbs of the umeni, it has been worth it.

Marek Fodor - President of Kantox

The happiest company in the world

They say that if a company is not doing well, the people who work in it won't be happy. It is fair to affirm that it works the opposite way: companies can only do well if the people who work in it are happy and are treated as an actual asset to the business. David Tomás tells it to us in the best way possible, placing people in the center and summarizing it in eleven keys of easy application.

Miquel Cabré - President of Abacus Cooperativa

© 2015, David Tomás
Translation: © Toni Crabb

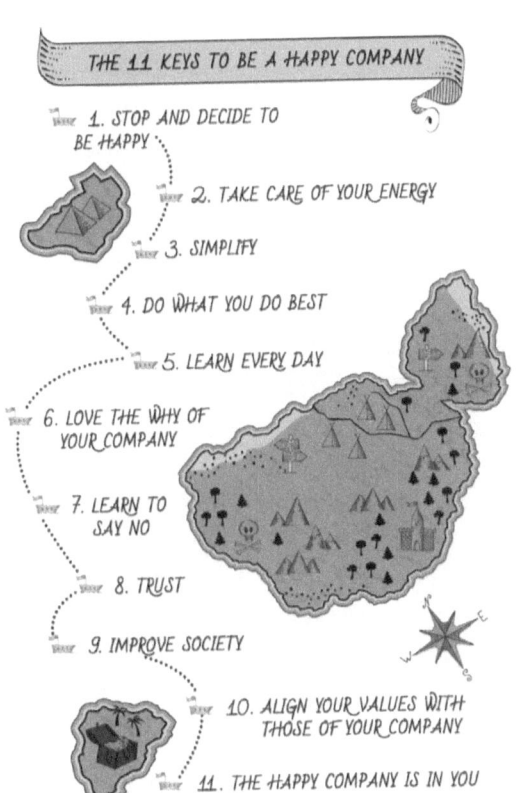

www.ingramcontent.com/pod-product-compliance
Lightning Source LLC
Chambersburg PA
CBHW030938240526
45463CB00015B/406